WADSWORTH PHILOSOPHERS

ON

KAROL WOJTYŁA

Peter Simpson
College of Staten Island

D1262013

WADSWORTH

— ✳ — ™

THOMSON LEARNING

Australia • Canada • Mexico • Singapore • Spain
United Kingdom • United States

To Robert A. Connor: Philosopher, Counselor, Friend

Printed in the United States of America
1 2 3 4 5 6 7 04 03 02 01 00

For permission to use material from this text, contact us:
Web: http://www.thomsonrights.com
Fax: 1-800-730-2215
Phone: 1-800-730-2214

For more information, contact:
Wadsworth/Thomson Learning, Inc.
10 Davis Drive
Belmont, CA 94002-3098
USA
http://www.wadsworth.com

ISBN: 0-534-58375-X

Table of Contents

Acknowledgements

I remember first reading the philosophy of Karol Wojtyła as presented in *The Acting Person* shortly after he was elected Pope in 1978. I also remember not really understanding what he was up to. I was able to make some sense of it, of course, but only by retranslating it into the ideas and terminology of St. Thomas Aquinas. Not until much later did I realize that by doing this I was almost entirely missing the point. Wojtyła was not trying to write Thomism in non-Thomistic language; he was trying to achieve a whole new perspective on the topic of the human person that went beyond, even if it also used, the achievements of St. Thomas. I have to thank Robert A. Connor for correcting these errors of my younger years. He it was who kept forcing me back to Wojtyła's writings, both philosophical and theological, and insisted, against my stubbornness and incomprehension, that there was something new and exciting going on. I have eventually come to agree with him and this book is in part the result. He will doubtless say that there are still things I am missing, but I think too that he will not be wholly dissatisfied. At any rate I owe him my warmest thanks for his help, patience, and unfailingly good-hearted advice. He well deserves to receive the dedication of this book.

I must also thank Daniel Kolak, the editor, and Wadsworth Press, the publisher, for having the courage and the open mindedness to include a book on Karol Wojtyła in their Wadsworth Philosophers Series. The less liberal minded might have balked, though unjustifiably as I hope this book will show, at the idea of setting a pope as a philosopher on a par with other philosophers. Kolak and Wadsworth Press did not and are to be commended accordingly. Others to be thanked for help and comments at various stages of this project are Yvonne Raley, Robert Talisse, and Helen Watt. Doubtless this book could be better than it is, but without their help it would have been worse.

New York City
September 2000

Abbreviations

The following abbreviations will be used to indicate the titles of Wojtyła's works within the parenthetical citations used in the text. Full bibliographical information is provided in the brief bibliography at the end of the text.

1

Life and Works of Karol Wojtyła

Life

Karol Wojtyła was born in 1920 in Wadowice in Poland. He was the third and last child of Emilia and Karol Wojtyła (there was a daughter who had died in infancy and another son Edmund). When the young Karol was only nine years old his mother, who had often been ill, died of kidney failure and congenital heart disease. This was not the last time that tragedy would strike the Wojtyła family. At any rate, Karol's father, who had recently retired on a captain's pension from the Polish army, did not remarry but devoted himself instead to bringing up his now motherless sons. Karol went to elementary and high school in Wadowice, and while at high school he developed an interest in acting and the theatre. This interest continued into his university years and attracted him for a time to an acting career. When Karol was about twelve, his brother Edmund, older by some fourteen years and now practicing as a medical doctor, contracted scarlet fever from one of his patients and himself died. Karol had grown very close to Edmund, and Edmund's death, following so quickly on that of his mother, must have been a hard blow for both Karol and his father.

When Karol had finished high school, his father moved to Cracow where Karol enrolled in the famous Jagiellonian University. The year was 1938. The following year on September 1 Hitler invaded Poland.

The country was quickly overrun and subjected to German control. The Jagiellonian University was closed down and most of the professors were deported to concentration camps where many of them died. Hitler wanted to crush Polish culture as well as Poland. Not surprisingly a cultural resistance sprang up to preserve that culture, and the young Karol joined it. The members would meet in private houses to read and perform the works of Polish literature. It was at this time that Karol himself began to write plays and have them performed for these meetings. Such resistance activity was dangerous. Detection would have meant immediate deportation to the concentration camps and probable death. There was danger on the streets too with random killings and roundups of young men by German patrols. Karol survived in part because he was employed as a manual laborer at a local chemical factory. It gave him a precious work card. But death struck anyway for in 1941 his father died of a heart attack. With this last of his immediate family gone the young Karol had never been so alone. He found some solace with a close friend in the cultural resistance whose family invited him into their own home. He was also soon able to resume his studies at the Jagiellonian University which had secretly been reconstituted by the resistance.

Karol was, of course, brought up Catholic and under the influence of his father, a man of deep prayer, Karol was earnest in his practice of the faith. The Germans had deported many of the priests to the camps and there were few priests left in the parishes to care for the spiritual needs of the people. Laymen were called on to help out. In Karol's parish one such layman was Jan Tyranowski, a tailor by profession but something of a theologian and a mystic too. He helped run discussion groups for the young people on all matters of theology and apologetics. In addition he organized them into "living rosaries." The rosary is a popular Catholic mode of prayer and consists of meditating on particular events, or "mysteries," in the life of Jesus and Mary. There are fifteen such mysteries and Tyranowski organized the young people into groups of fifteen to form the living rosary. The members of each group pledged to help each other in all areas of their life and above all in the pursuit of Christian perfection.

All this had its effect on the young Wojtyła and in 1942 he decided to study for the priesthood. The Archbishop of Cracow, Cardinal Sapieha, had realized that training a new generation of priests, to replace those who had been deported and killed in the camps, was going to be vital for the future of the Polish Church and nation. He set up an underground seminary where Wojtyła, after his days of hard manual labor, would study philosophy and later theology. Toward the end of the German occupation the seminarians were all moved into the Archbishop's residence to protect them from being rounded up or shot by the Germans, who were increasingly desperate in the face of the Soviet advance. Wojtyła had himself to dodge German patrols in his escape to the residence. He was there when the Germans were finally driven out of Poland and the Soviet controlled Communists took over. The Communists proved themselves little friendlier to the Church than the Nazis, but they did allow some semblance of normal life to resume. At all events Wojtyła was ordained a priest by Cardinal Sapieha in 1946 and was immediately sent to Rome to study for a doctorate in theology. He completed this doctorate in 1948 with a dissertation on the mysticism of St. John of the Cross (a topic perhaps inspired by Wojtyła's association with Tyranowski). He then spent some time in France studying the Catholic workers' movement before returning to Cracow where he took up pastoral duties.

Wojtyła had a real talent for pastoral work and spiritual counseling, especially of young students, and he enjoyed it a great deal. He would have preferred to stay doing such work but in 1951 Cardinal Sapieha died and his successor, Archbishop Baziak, decided that Wojtyła should prepare for an academic vocation. He sent Wojtyła to study for his *habilitation* (a sort of second doctorate required to qualify as a university teacher) at the Jagiellonian University. Wojtyła wrote a dissertation on the moral philosophy of Max Scheler, a phenomenologist and student of Husserl, who was to have a profound influence on the development of his own moral philosophy later. Wojtyła completed his doctorate in 1954 and was ready to take up a position in the Faculty of Theology at the Jagiellonian University when the Communists closed the Faculty down. Wojtyła was invited instead by one of the readers of his dissertation to take up a position teaching ethics at the University of Lublin and, with the permission of Archbishop Baziak, Wojtyła agreed. Within two years he succeeded to the Chair of Ethics, and held the post, fulfilling its duties despite increasing ecclesiastical responsibilities, for the next twenty two years.

In 1958 Wojtyła was made an auxiliary bishop to Archbishop Baziak. In 1962 Baziak died and Wojtyła was elected by the senior priests of the archdiocese to act as administrator until a successor should be named. It was in this capacity that he first attended the Second Vatican Council which held its opening session in that same year. In late 1963 Pope Paul VI named Wojtyła Archbishop of Cracow and he was installed in March of 1964. In 1967 the pope elevated him to the College of Cardinals. Finally, in October 1978, he was himself elected pope and took the name of John Paul II.

Wojtyła's election as pope brought him to worldwide attention. It also brought to worldwide attention the fact that he was a professor of philosophy and author of original works in philosophy. Without that election his philosophy would have been known in Poland and in some more specialized scholarly circles, but one wonders if it would have penetrated much further. I do not mean by this to cast any doubts on the value of that philosophy. On the contrary, it is a philosophy of much merit that well deserves to be studied in its own right. I merely wish to say that what deserves to be noticed sometimes only gets noticed because of incidental historical events. In Wojtyła's case the event was his election to the papacy. Because of it his philosophy has attracted interest, not only for its own sake as it deserves, but also because of how it might help people understand the mind of a man who, since his election, has been striding the world like a colossus. For that reason alone, if for no other, the thought of this erstwhile professor of philosophy deserves to be made accessible to as wide a readership as possible.

Works

The strictly philosophical works of Karol Wojtyła can be reduced to two main books and numerous scholarly articles. The books are a work on ethics and marriage published in 1960 and translated in English as *Love and Responsibility*, and a work on the philosophy of man or philosophical anthropology published in 1969 and translated in English as *The Acting Person*. This latter is undoubtedly the more important. Wojtyła's scholarly articles appeared in various philosophical journals during the years that he was professor at Lublin. Many of these articles have now been collected and translated into English by Theresa Sandok in an excellent volume entitled *Person and Community*. There are in addition Wojtyła's two dissertations, one on St. John of the Cross and the other on Max Scheler, only the first of which is currently available in English.

Wojtyła also wrote a number of more properly theological works, and notably a book on the teaching of the Second Vatican Council published in 1972 and translated in English as *Sources of Renewal*. In addition, since his election as pope, Wojtyła has produced a large number of theological writings, official and unofficial, of which the

4

most important are the thirteen papal encyclicals. Wojtyła's theological writings are closely connected to his philosophy and some treatment of them is necessary to give a full picture of his thinking. However the focus of the present book must be Wojtyła's philosophy.

I have divided the book into four parts. The first part in chapter two concentrates on Wojtyła's philosophical articles so that, through them, readers may get a good idea of his basic philosophical stance. This stance is original to Wojtyła and was achieved through a novel appropriation and fusion of traditional scholasticism (in particular Thomism) and phenomenology. It is necessary to get as clear as possible about the nature and sources of this stance if one is to understand the results that Wojtyła achieved through it in his two major philosophical works and also in his theology.

Of the two major philosophical works *The Acting Person*, although written after *Love and Responsibility*, is logically prior to it. For it deals with the fundamental anthropology that Wojtyła has developed while *Love and Responsibility* deals with that anthropology's ethical application and development. True, *Love and Responsibility* does, especially in its opening chapters, contain some statement of the anthropology, but it does not go into it thoroughly and in detail. There is good reason, therefore, to begin an exposition of the substance of Wojtyła's philosophy with *The Acting Person* and not with *Love and Responsibility*. Accordingly chapter three deals with the former work and chapter four with the latter. Chapter five deals with the theological writings insofar as these reflect, and indeed reveal, the philosophy.

One point, however, about *The Acting Person* needs to be clarified at the outset. The English translation of this work, unlike the English translations of Wojtyła's other works, has been clouded by controversy. The translation was actually made from a revision of the Polish edition prepared by the author. The English translation is thus, in principle, more up to date and accurate than what first appeared in Polish. However the editor of it, Anna-Teresa Tymieniecka, introduced a number of rewordings of her own into the English of the translator, Andrzej Potocki, and controversy has arisen as to whether the author's thought has after all been correctly conveyed. The dispute concerns whether these rewordings have not made the work appear more phenomenological than it really is and thereby obscured the extent to which it still assumes and uses scholastic terminology and ideas.

A particular case in point is the Latin term *suppositum* which is used in scholastic metaphysics, and by Wojtyła himself, to indicate the real objective being of the subject it is applied to, which in this instance is the human subject, the human person. The English of *The Acting Person* does not use the word *suppositum* while this word is used extensively in the Polish original. In its place the English says things like "the structural/ontological basis" or "the concrete ontological nucleus of man" (Buttiglione, 117n; Kalinowski, 201-203; Weigel, 174n, 880 n83). However, appearances notwithstanding, these changes do not pose any serious problem to English readers of Wojtyła's thought. First, the term *suppositum*, along with other scholastic terms, is used everywhere in the English translation of Wojtyła's articles, and *The Acting Person*, when read in the light of these articles (which is anyway desirable, if not even necessary, for understanding that work), can be seen, despite the difference of wording, to be saying exactly the same thing and to be upholding exactly the same doctrine. Second, the wording of the translation, while not traditional, is not misleading either if it is properly weighed. The flavor of the English may thus be less scholastic than the Polish, but the substance hardly is.

In short, I conclude that, if his philosophical writings in English translation are taken fairly and in their totality, there is no good reason to suppose that Wojtyła's authentic thought is not fully accessible to English speaking readers.

2

The Philosophical 'Prise de Position'

Thematizing the Human Person

When approaching and explaining the thought of any philosopher, the first and perhaps the most important task is to determine where to begin. In the case of some philosophers this can be rather hard (I think of Hegel, for instance, or Nietzsche). In the case of Karol Wojtyła it is relatively easy. Continuing on from that beginning is, to be sure, not at all easy, as it is not with most philosophers, but that beginning itself comes readily enough to view. For there is one idea or object that runs through the whole of Wojtyła's work like an ever recurring theme, the theme of the human person. Many variations are played on this theme as his thought progresses but it remains always beneath or within them as the enduring subject. Indeed Wojtyła has, in a sense, written about nothing else. His writing, even indeed as John Paul II, has been one long meditation on man. To say this is not to say or imply anything narrow or negative. The theme of man, especially as Wojtyła treats of it, is a richly absorbing topic. Indeed the effort to explore it has taken Wojtyła himself into almost every part of philosophy (and perhaps theology too). It has become, as it were, a light to illumine the whole of reality.

Wojtyła's preoccupation with the question of man, as opposed to that of being, say, or consciousness or knowledge, may in part be due

7

to certain facts of his personal history. Few questions could, perhaps, have been more insistently forced on the attention of a reflective young Pole come to manhood in the middle years of the Twentieth Century than the question of man. For Poland, like many another unfortunate country of Eastern Europe, was crushed by two brutal tyrannies one after the other, Nazism and Communism. In both cases the capacity of man to sink to the level of a beast or rise to that of an angel must have been a matter of all too present observation. Nazism and Communism, however, were not just tyrannies, on a par perhaps with ancient tyrannies save for the greater brutality made possible by modern technology. They were also ideologies. They were built on and enforced, as a matter of policy, a distinctive view of man. To oppose these tyrannies, if only in one's desires and thoughts, was to oppose a philosophy of man. It was perforce, therefore, to have or at least to want another and different philosophy of man.

Moreover it was not just the facts of Nazism and Communism in Eastern Europe that would force the necessity of reflection. The West too, with which Wojtyła was familiar through early studies in Italy and France, must have borne in on him the same problem, if for different reasons. For to the materialism of Marxist ideology in the East could be counterposed the materialism of the emerging consumer societies in the West. These too put all their focus on the "quantitative development" of man's condition and paid little attention to the person of man himself (*AP:* 21-22).

As Wojtyła himself wrote later in 1976:

> The present age...is a time of great controversy about the human being, controversy about the very meaning of human existence, and thus about the nature and significance of the human being...This aptly describes the situation in Poland today with respect to the whole reality that has arisen out of Marxism, out of dialectical materialism, and strives to win minds over to this ideology...After nearly twenty years of ideological debate in Poland, it has become clear that at the center of this debate is not cosmology or philosophy of nature but philosophical anthropology and ethics: the great and fundamental controversy about the human being. ('The Person: Subject and Community,' *PC:* 220)

This quotation actually leads us to a deeper and ultimately more significant factor in Wojtyła's thinking than the history of the

Twentieth Century or than the history of Wojtyła himself. It is one to which he himself repeatedly draws attention in his philosophical writings, I mean the history of Western Philosophy. For there is in this history a divide or fissure that appears at the beginning of what we nowadays call the modern period (the period beginning with Descartes). Wojtyła characterizes this fissure as a division between the philosophy of being, which is characteristic of Aristotle and Aquinas and of ancient and medieval philosophy generally, and the philosophy of consciousness, which is characteristic of philosophy since Descartes. Descartes initiated a turn of philosophy inward to the self and the self's own subjective awareness of its cognitive acts, and to the presence of objects of knowledge within consciousness. Descartes' insistence on beginning all knowledge with knowledge of myself and of my consciousness marks a clear turn away from the objective stance of the pre-Cartesian tradition, which had focused, by contrast, on the externally existing being of things and indeed on this being of man too insofar as he is some sort of natural thing ('Subjectivity and the Irreducible in the Human Being,' *PC:* 209-10, 216; 'Thomistic Personalism,' *PC:* 169-71; 'The Problem of the Theory of Morality,' *PC:* 158-59).

A striking indication of this difference can be found in the definitions of man given in the Aristotelian tradition on the one hand and by Descartes on the other. In the Aristotelian tradition, man is a natural thing alongside other natural things; he is an animal of a certain sort, a rational animal. This is, as Wojtyła expresses it, a cosmological approach to man, a way of seeing him from the point of view of the cosmos as a whole. It is a way of seeing him as a particular part of that cosmos and so as something ultimately reducible to it ('Subjectivity and the Irreducible in the Human Being,' *PC:* 211-15). For Descartes, by contrast, man is essentially the "I think" of conscious cognitive states and precisely not so reducible. Talk of rationality and animality in this regard is, indeed, positively misleading; it misses that about man which is peculiar to him and that sets him apart from the mass of extended things in the world. For these latter (among which man, viewed as an extended animal body, is included) could, as far external experience is concerned, be just sorts of machines or automata. They would lack any interior life, any lived experience of the "I think" or "I am conscious." But it is precisely this "I think" and not any rational animality that makes the individual human being, the real conscious self, to be what it is. What Descartes thus discovered, or perhaps recovered, and what gave modern philosophy its special impetus, was the subjectivity, the interiority, of the human person. It is man as a conscious subject or as a consciousness that becomes the focus of distinctively post-Cartesian philosophy.

Wojtyła regards this turn towards the person, and to the subjectivity and inwardness of the person, as a fundamentally positive and necessary development that must be embraced and pursued. He regards it moreover as fundamentally compatible with, and supplementary to, the older and more objective approach of the philosophy of being. Both this latter approach and that of the modern philosophy of consciousness are needed to develop a comprehensive philosophical anthropology and ethics, and therefore to confront and answer the question of the human being that contemporary life so insistently poses.

There are nevertheless dangers in the philosophy of consciousness as it has developed from Descartes. The chief danger is that of subjectivism, of hypostatizing consciousness and making it into a subject all by itself without grounding it in anything further. This was already present in Descartes, and it leads to the positing of an absolute consciousness that freely creates its own world for itself and is not measured by any objective reality supposedly independent of it ('Thomistic Personalism,' *PC:* 169-70; 'The Human Person and Natural Law,' *PC:* 185; 'The Person: Subject and Community,' *PC:* 234). One response to this danger would be to reject the philosophy of consciousness altogether and confine oneself to the traditional philosophy of being. This, however, is not Wojtyła's response. If man is the great question of our day, and if the philosophy of consciousness has opened up new perspectives on that question (however exaggerated the claims made on behalf of these perspectives may sometimes be), then the philosophy of consciousness must be enlisted in the task of answering that question ('The Person: Subject and Community,' *PC:* 228).

Finding the Right Method

The clue as to how to do this, or how to use the philosophy of consciousness without falling into its exaggerations and errors is, for Wojtyła, to be found in the modern philosophy of phenomenology. This philosophy derives from the work of Edmund Husserl and, without going into unnecessary detail, one may say that what Husserl helped to uncover was a way to overcome the absolutizing of consciousness from within the philosophy of consciousness itself. A fundamental feature of Husserl's philosophy is the insistence on seeing consciousness in its totality, on letting all the rich givenness of the self's experience come to view, and not on paying attention to some features and not others or on privileging some features and downplaying others. Husserl's slogan of "back to the things themselves" or "back to the object" is indicative of this insistence. It meant going back to the things in all the fullness with which they presented themselves to consciousness. Perhaps the first and chief result of doing this, and one stressed by phenomenology, is that the objects of consciousness are *transcendent* to consciousness, and that they are so because (cognitive) acts of consciousness are *intentional*. By intentional is meant that these acts display a directedness from the subject toward an object. They are not focused on themselves but on some object beyond themselves. This object is, as such, not reducible to the subjective conscious acts of which it is the object. It *transcends* them.

Another and perhaps clearer way of putting this is to say that there is an inescapable objectivism to consciousness and its acts, so much so that a reduction of consciousness to subjectivism (as was already implicit in Descartes, who ignored the intentional or transcendent character of cognized objects) is necessarily mistaken. For even if the objects known in a given act are ideal as opposed to real, or abstract as opposed to concrete, they are nevertheless, relative to the act, objects transcendent to the act ('The Problem of the Separation of Experience from the Act in Ethics,' *PC:* 34, 51). Such a position is not yet objectivist in the sense of realist (for the objects of consciousness might not, for all their intentional transcendence, have any real existence independently of consciousness), but the step from the first to the second is short. Objects known in consciousness but transcendent to the act of being known are certainly the sorts of thing (unlike Descartes' Ideas) that could really exist independently of their being known. There is some doubt as to whether Husserl firmly took the step to realism, or whether he took it and then stepped back again into subjectivism and idealism; but it is certain that several of his students did. Among these was Max Scheler, whose thinking, especially in ethics, exercised a considerable influence on Wojtyła, as will be discussed shortly.

At all events the phenomenology that Wojtyła adopts in his investigations of the human person is realist phenomenology, a phenomenology that does not construct or constitute everything out of an absolute and free-standing consciousness, but that discovers in consciousness, or conscious experience, the objective reality of real

11

things and real people. Conscious experience, because of its intentional character, is experience of a real, external world, and is itself the act or experience of a real human subject. Wojtyła turns to phenomenology as a way to get at this subject from within, to grasp it in its interiority as a conscious self. But that this self is first a real being in the world, in direct contact with other beings in the world, is never matter for doubt (*AP:* 8-10, 19, 21).

Part of Wojtyła's reasoning here is that the objective reality of the self as a personal subject is an immediate given of that subject's own experience. This is one of the achievements of the phenomenological method. A full and unbiased looking at conscious experience is sufficient, Wojtyła insists, to reveal that the subject having the experience and the objects experienced are real beings and not mere modifications of consciousness ('The Personal Structure of Self-Determination,' *PC:* 188-89; 'The Person: Subject and Community,' *PC:* 221-23). If one were to object here that this begs the question or is bare assertion on Wojtyła's part (for what if I say my experience is not like that, or what if I simply deny his claims?), then the only response could be to urge a return, unbiased by any prior conceptions, back to conscious experience, or back to the things themselves in all their self-given reality. There is, if you like, a question here of a basic honesty as to what one does actually experience. Experience and only experience is the bottom line, beyond which there can be no more basic authority and from which there can be no further appeal. What experience is like and what it is experience of are themselves matters of experience, not of proof from some supposedly more basic premises. There are no premises more basic than experience. Aristotle had already made that point (*Metaphysics* 1011a3-16; *On Generation and Corruption*, 325a13-23), and Wojtyła follows him in his own way (*AP:* 9-10, 15). If some still want to object then, says Wojtyła in effect, let experience take care of them. Our task is to get on with the understanding of experience as it really is and not to keep circling back to respond to those who, despite every appeal, go on rejecting its evidence.

Wojtyła's fundamental realism, however, is not only a matter of his being true in this way to the phenomenology of experience. It meets and unites with the fundamental realism of scholastic (and Thomistic) ontology. Wojtyła is a scholastic realist and a phenomenologist at the same time, and he is perhaps one because he is the other. There is a real symbiosis or cross-fertilization of the two traditions in his thought. The way to grasp this fact, and indeed the way to see what Wojtyła's philosophy is about, is to focus on that very objective reality of the human subject which he himself so stresses. For as soon as one does this one meets what the scholastics called the *suppositum*. 'Suppositum' is a term to signify the being of the individual thing. It expresses the fact that any actual individual of any nature or species is a self-subsistent reality existing as such in its own right. Fido the dog and Felix the cat are really existing individuals or supposita; they are concrete realizations of dog-nature and cat-nature respectively. Dog-nature and cat-nature do not exist in separation. There is no Dog-in-Itself or Cat-in-Itself existing somewhere (that would be Platonism); they exist only as concretized in a particular suppositum, a particular individual. Conversely, every suppositum is the locus of a concretized nature, or it is the sort of suppositum it is because of the nature which it has—Fido having the nature of dogness and Felix of catness ('Thomistic Personalism, *PC:* 167; 'The Human Person and Natural Law,' *PC:* 182; 'The Problem of Catholic Sexual Ethics,' *PC:* 284). Of course, Wojtyła's focus is on the human suppositum not on supposita generally, and his analyses are all analyses of the being and lived experience of the human suppositum. Still, it is important to stress, and to keep in mind, that human beings are supposita, real existents in the concrete, material world. They are not Cartesian consciousnesses cut off from external things and closed up within their own subjective egos. Wojtyła is never tempted to buy into the idealism or subjectivism of the philosophy of consciousness. He is never tempted to give up the objective reality of individual persons. He remains, in this regard, at one with the pre-Cartesian tradition of ancient and medieval philosophy. Whatever else one may ultimately say about the modernity or novelty of Wojtyła's thinking, one must always keep in mind the uncompromising scholastic realism that lies at the bottom of it. Wojtyła is trying to combine philosophies, not to reject one in favor of the other (*AP:* xiii-xiv, 19-21, 80; 'The Person: Subject and Community,' *PC:* 222-25; 'Subjectivity and the Irreducible in the Human Being,' *PC:* 212-16).

Lived Experience

With the realism of the idea of suppositum in place, Wojtyła turns, in his efforts to understand the particular supposita that are human, to the resources provided by phenomenology. One might wonder why he chooses this path rather than rests content with the method and discoveries, by no means trivial or outdated, of the same scholasticism from which he drew the idea of the suppositum. The

The Philosophical 'Prise de Position' answer is to be found in what Wojtyła, following the phenomenological tradition, calls "lived experience." By this is meant more or less what was just mentioned, namely the immediate givens of the subject's own experience taken in all their unbiased fullness. But one has to proceed with a certain caution at this point because of the relative novelty of what Wojtyła has in mind. Lived experience, he says, is a category foreign to the metaphysics of Aristotle and therewith also of scholasticism. It is not indeed contrary to that metaphysics, but it is not focused on or thematized or, better, "paused at" in that metaphysics. Rather Aristotle's metaphysics passes over it in its reductive effort to see and place the human being in the external world as a thing alongside other things. This reduction is neither wrong nor undesirable. On the contrary it is necessary. But, in the light of the history of modern philosophy and of the problem of man in the present age, it is not enough. One must instead, in the process of the reduction, pause at the "irreducible" in man, at that which makes each man unique and unrepeatable. Of course, any individual of any species is, qua this individual, unique and unrepeatable. But the individual man is more than an individual of a certain species. He is a personal subject, a conscious self, the self that has been massively thematized by modern philosophy but relatively ignored by the traditional philosophy of being ('Subjectivity and the Irreducible in the Human Being,' *PC:* 209-17).

One might ask, however, given that the lived experience of the human person is not supposed to be a category of metaphysics, how and where it comes into the ontological picture. If it is a being or part of being, it must be part of ontology. If it is not, it cannot come to objective view and we slip back into idealism or subjectivism. What one should perhaps say, then, in response to this is that Wojtyła's shift to the personalistic perspective, or to the philosophy of consciousness, is less a shift to some unknown metaphysical category as a shift to a different "dimension" within existing categories. I mean it is a shift to the dimension opened up by taking seriously what it is to be a self-conscious suppositum when that suppositum is viewed from the suppositum's own inner experience of itself.

The point here seems to be as follows. In traditional metaphysical terms, the human suppositum is a substance, and its powers and acts and self-awareness (its "lived experience") are properties ("accidents") of that substance. They do not define or constitute what it is, but they can and do express or reveal what it is ('The Person: Subject and Community,' *PC:* 227, 231; 'Thomistic Personalism,' *PC:* 169-71; *AP:* 45-46, 96). Now it is this expressing or revealing that, we may say,

14

Wojtyła wants to explore, and to explore from within because, indeed, the human suppositum, in its lived reality, is precisely a "within." Ordinarily, or as regards other beings in the world like trees or horses, the activity proper to the particular thing—as nutrition, growth, reproduction, resting, moving—proceeds outward from the thing into its immediate environment or into other material parts of itself. But in the case of the thing that is a human being, its acts do not just proceed outward like this; they also return back into the subject in a special way. They become *mirrored* and reflected in the subject's own consciousness. The subject does not just act or get acted upon; it experiences itself acting and being acted upon and does so immediately. The subject, in being conscious of itself, thus comes, in a way, to possess itself. In fact it thus first comes to be or to be constituted as a *self*. For the very idea of a self betokens self-awareness, or betokens self-reflexivity. Man is a self in this sense while plants and minerals and animals are not. Or if some of the higher primates possibly are, this seems only to be in some primitive and inchoate way. At all events we know that man is a self and to such a degree as to indicate a difference in kind of selfhood. It is this unique and special kind of selfhood that is and must be the focus for Wojtyła, concerned, as he is, with the question and the phenomenon of man in modern thought and experience.

The self, then, which thus comes to view in lived experience and which is, in a way, constituted through lived experience, is neither substance nor accident but the two fused together, as it were, in a single experience of self-possession. Let me explain. The self that possesses and the self that is possessed are not simply one self, but also a self that is a self-subsistent suppositum (a substance) coming back to itself in acts (accidents) of immediate self-awareness, or *reflexivity* as Wojtyła calls it (the non-intentional presence of the self to itself in its natural turning back on itself; *AP:* 42-45). For it is one's very self, one's very being, that one possesses through this self-awareness, and not merely some transient or even permanent activities and states. To be sure, one can, through an effort of metaphysical abstraction, distinguish this immediate experience of self-possession into its constituent categories (substance and accident). But that is not how the experience of self-possession is itself given to us. It is given as a unity. That may help to explain, in fact, why so many philosophers of consciousness took it as a real unity and subjectivized consciousness into pure consciousness, denying its groundedness in the objective reality of the suppositum. But this, insists Wojtyła, is an error, an error discernible from within that experience itself. The subjective self-subsistence of the self in the real human suppositum is a given of that experience. One must not, therefore, let it go. Yet at the same time one must not slip immediately back into the metaphysical abstractions that, considered cosmologically or ontologically, it necessarily points to. One must, without forgetting the subsistent reality of the self, *pause at the irreducible*, at the unique presence of the self to itself in lived experience.

To put the point in Wojtyła's own words:

> Objectivity belongs to the essence of experience, and so the human being, who is that subject, is also given in experience in an objective way. Experience, so to speak, dispels the notion of "pure consciousness"…

> By "metaphysical" I mean not so much "beyond-the-phenomenal" as "through the phenomenal" or "trans-phenomenal." Through all the phenomena that in experience go to make up the whole human being as someone who exists and acts, we perceive—somehow we must perceive—the subject of that existence and activity. Or better, we perceive that the human being is—must be—that subject ('The Person: Subject and Community,' *PC:* 221-23).

We may say, then, that the suppositum, the real individual substance that each man is, is itself directly given in our experience of ourselves; it is taken up into that experience and becomes part of it. The suppositum is not something beyond experience that, in some Kantian transcendental way, has to be presupposed to experience and is never given in experience. Rather it is something that is immediately present in all experience—not indeed as another phenomenal episode (that would be to fall back into subjectivism) but as the abiding subject of phenomena that enters into the being of phenomena and is therefore necessarily experienced through the phenomena. It is what gives ontological consistency, as it were, to the self that is man and prevents him from being dissolved into mere episodes of consciousness. Wojtyła's notion of "lived experience," or the fusion (as I earlier called it) of the substantial and accidental, is thus in a way his fundamental (and traditional) realism all over again. Only now it is understood from the "inside" of our own subjective experience of ourselves and not from the "outside" of objective metaphysical analysis. Metaphysical subjectivity—the ontological reality of the suppositum—is transferred into, or manifested as, personal subjectivity—the interior, experienced givenness of myself to myself ('The Person: Subject and Community,' *PC:* 225).

Wojtyła also puts the point in another way: "Being a subject (a suppositum) and experiencing oneself as a subject occur on two entirely different dimensions." It is the latter dimension, of course, that gives us contact with the actual reality of the self (one can *be* a supppositum, for instance, while asleep, but one cannot *experience* oneself thus); and it is consciousness that plays the constitutive role here. Consciousness is what makes the human suppositum a human *self:* "The self is constituted through the mediation of consciousness in the suppositum humanum within the context of the whole existence (*esse*) and activity (*operari*) proper to this suppositum" ('The Person: Subject and Community,' *PC:* 227; *AP:* 44).

There is present here a distinction between "suppositum" and "self," or to quote Wojtyła again:

> The self is nothing other than the concrete suppositum humanum which, when given to itself by consciousness (self-consciousness) in the lived experience of action, is identical with…self-possession and self-governance…The lived experience of our personal subjectivity is simply the full actualization of all that is contained virtually in our metaphysical subjectivity (suppositum humanum)…The suppositum humanum and the human self are but two poles of one and the same experience of the human being ('The Person: Subject and Community,' *PC:* 231-32).

In other words, the concept of the suppositum, taken precisely as such (that is, as a *metaphysical* subject) does not yet bring to light the full richness of the being of that suppositum, namely that it is a *personal self.* Only in lived experience, in reflexive consciousness and deliberate action, does the self both come to light and, in a sense, also come to be. The self after all, says Wojtyła as already quoted above, "is constituted through the mediation of consciousness in the suppositum." The self, we may say, is none other than the suppositum come to itself through a sort of re-creation of itself in its own self-conscious activity. Such a reality can, of course, be reduced to the metaphysical categories of substance and accident. But before one does that one can pause at it and take it for what it is in its own dimension as lived experience. That, at any rate, is what Wojtyła tries to do, and in doing so he does not take himself to be do anything contrary to the traditional philosophy of being. To this extent he would seem to be right. After all, since we do manifestly have an inner life, a life constituted by and in our conscious selves, we can certainly look at this interior life as it is given to us in our experience of it. And we can use it to come to an understanding, perhaps a richer understanding, of who and what we are. Certainly someone seized by the problem of man, and especially of modern man, cannot but seize in his turn the chance to come at it in different ways or from different angles. And all the more so if these ways are peculiarly modern ways that lie at the heart of that problem.

The Issue of Efficacy

The modern philosophy of consciousness focuses on *cognitive* aspects or acts and understands the self primarily in *cognitive* terms (as is already very clear in Descartes). The absolutizing of consciousness and the subjectivism into which that philosophy almost immediately falls are an absolutizing and a subjectivizing of the self as *cognitive* consciousness. Even the recovery of the object within the philosophy of phenomenology (through its prior recovery of the idea of intentionality) is a recovery of objectivity in cognitive acts. Consciousness is said to be consciousness of something transcendent to consciousness in the sense of the intended and intentional object of acts of knowing and awareness. This was an important recovery and it led the way back to an authentic realism, especially in the early period of phenomenology and in the work of several of Husserl's students. It is this same realism of the object of cognitive consciousness, of course, that Wojtyła has also used to recover the suppositum of the philosophy of being within the philosophy of consciousness. But the human person is not only a cognitive being. He is an affective and active being, a being that feels and loves and values. Subjectivism and the absolutizing of consciousness impede the understanding of the person in the case of action and value as much as they do in the case of cognition. The subjectivism of value, indeed, is perhaps more at the center of the contemporary human problem than the subjectivism of cognition. It is certainly at the center of the relativism in ethics and politics that we find so prevalent today.

The recovery of a certain objective realism in the sphere of values from within the modern philosophy of consciousness was achieved by Max Scheler. Wojtyła was much influenced by Scheler and found in him a powerful stimulus for his own reflections about the person. What particularly impressed him was how Scheler, against the prevailing formalism of Kantian ethics, reestablished the fact and the reality of moral value, or of moral goods, as objective givens of personal, lived experience. For Kant there are no such goods or values given to us in experience. The only goods or values we do experience are the pleasures of subjective happiness and are too low or too self-interested to be a basis for morality. Morality must instead be founded on the categorical imperative which stresses duty, or obedience to a free-standing 'ought' or norm, and not any concrete and cognizable value. Scheler rejects this and claims instead that phenomenological reflection on one's own experience shows the presence there of genuinely moral values, of goods that are not the goods of self-interested pleasure. Moral values are, like cognized objects, given in the intentional acts of the personal subject; only in this case the acts are *affective* and not cognitive. Values, in other words, are, for Scheler, the real objects of our intentional, affective acts and, as such, no less real and objective than the objects of cognition. This move of Scheler's is a decisive one for the philosophy of consciousness in overcoming subjectivism and formalism in ethics, and Wojtyła welcomes it as such. It brings us back to the fullness of experienced reality (just as the recognition of the suppositum as a real subject, and object, of conscious acts brings us back to the fullnes of experienced reality).

Nevertheless Wojtyła sees two defects in Scheler's analysis. The first and less important of these is that the intentional acts in which value is experienced are ones of emotion or affectivity alone and not also of knowledge. As far as Scheler is concerned, reason only grasps the thing-like structure of objects; the value element of objective reality, by contrast, is grasped in emotional experience, whether the experience of love or of hate. For Wojtyła this is not only a mistake in itself (for he accepts the traditional ancient and medieval claim that reason grasps the good of things and not just their factual being; 'The Problem of the Will in the Analysis of the Ethical Act,' *PC:* 5, 14-15); it contributes also to a second and, in the end, worse mistake. This worse mistake is the failure to realize that what primarily characterizes ethical experience, and therefore what a true phenomenology should bring especially to light, is the *efficacy* or *agency* of the acting person. Ethical experience is above all the experience that I am a cause of my own acts and, indeed, of the fact that they are good or bad acts. It is in the will and willing that ethical reality comes to the fore. It does not come to the fore, then, in the mere registering of values in intentional acts of emotion, but rather in the response to, and in the realization of, values in one's own self-caused acts. In other words, in addition to what Wojtyła elsewhere calls the "horizontal" transcendence typical of intentional acts of awareness or affectivity, we need the "vertical" transcendence of self-realization in acts of willing and doing wherein *we determine ourselves* to choose and carry out the values we recognize (*AP:* viii, xiii; 'The Problem of the Separation of Experience from the Act in Ethics,' *PC:* 27-28, 33-36; 'In Search of the Basis of Perfectionism in Ethics,' *PC:* 49-53).

This failure to recognize or focus upon personal efficacy or agency in action is found, says Wojtyła, not only in Scheler but also in Kant, despite the large differences that otherwise separate Kant's ethics from Scheler's. Actually Wojtyła finds in Kant's notion of duty a potentially more suggestive source for the recovery of agency than in Scheler's notion of value. For duty and the categorical imperative are, as such, a sort of summons to action. Unfortunately according to Kant, however, the actions that could be or are genuine responses to this summons are not part of concrete ethical experience. They belong rather to what is never given in experience, namely to the noumenal (that is, non-phenomenal and non-experiential) sphere of freedom and pure practical reason. There is, to be sure, an idea of agency here, but it is not an agency that we can experience in ourselves. The concrete or experienceable self is excluded from the realm of true or authentic ethical action. What is in fact given in experience is not act or agency but feeling, the feeling of awe or respect generated in us by the categorical command of duty. Such a feeling, if properly nourished, can confirm or deepen in us the experience of the command or of duty, but that is as far as it goes. It does not bring us into the experience of ethical agency, or the experience of our actually causing and bringing about ethical acts. Such causality is always noumenal and trans-empirical. It is a theoretical posit; not a part of lived experience. Hence, as far as actual ethical experience goes, Kant ends up on the same side as Scheler, with merely emotional states. The fact that for Scheler these emotional states are responses to material values (objects of experience) while for Kant they are a response to the pure form of duty and the categorical imperative makes no difference. For both Scheler and Kant have lost, or failed to recognize, the real agency or efficacy of the human person in ethical action. They have, in other words, for their different reasons, failed to look ethical experience full in the face and see it whole. A true phenomenology, by contrast, one that does genuinely go back to the things themselves, would see it whole ('The

Problem of the Separation of Experience from the Act in Ethics,' *PC:* 26, 29-32, 34; 'In Search of the Basis of Perfectionism in Ethics,' *PC:* 49-50; 'The Problem of the Will in the Analysis of the Ethical Act,' *PC:* 4-5, 8).

Wojtyła attributes the failure of Kant and Scheler in this regard to the fact that they both divorce human consciousness from the objective human *being*, that they do not see that the complete human being is a being, an active and causing being, and not just a consciousness. The philosophy of being, by contrast, did not make this mistake but retained a full sense of the importance of agency for the understanding of ethical reality. In other words, as before, the failure of Kant and Scheler is a failure to locate consciousness in the real human suppositum, the real human person, who exists alongside other real supposita. Wojtyła's fundamental scholastic realism thus comes back to the fore. It forms an indispensable basis for his reflections on the person, for his creative appropriation of the phenomenological method and of the philosophy of consciousness ('In Search of the Basis of Perfectionism in Ethics,' *PC:* 55).

Actually it was not only scholastic metaphysics that was decisive here. Wojtyła also found inspiration (and support) for his realism about the person in the work of certain experimental psychologists. For what they too discovered in their research, and quite independently of any allegiance to metaphysics, was the reality of agency, the actual fact-ness of efficacious willing and acting in people's experience. Denials or dismissals of such experience of agency (such as one finds in Kant and Scheler) run counter to experience and to the science of experimental psychology which investigates experience. A true account of the human person, and therefore a true response to the crisis of man in the modern age, cannot be achieved without a full, unbiased recovery of the efficacy of the human person. What experimental psychology has established here receives the full backing of, and in its own turn supports, the traditional metaphysics of being found in Aristotle and Aquinas. Man is a real being who in his equally real and experientially given agency actualizes himself in his acts. Man is thus a dynamic being, and such dynamism can only be understood on the basis of the philosophy of being, namely, in this case, the metaphysics of *potency* and *act*. When something or someone changes, say from cold to hot or from bad to good, what is happening is that the *potential* to be hot or good is getting realized in *actually* being hot or good. The philosophy of being is able to recognize this reality of motion, change, and action, even from within conscious experience, because it discerns in their essential structure the passage from potency to act, or the actual realization of an existing potential to be realized. Thus conscious human *action* is itself part of experience because it is, as a real passage from potency to act within the person's own faculties, as much a part of self-experience as any other conscious reality within the person ('The Problem of the Will in the Analysis of the Ethical Act,' *PC:* 3-22).

Nevertheless, such dynamism, while it can be understood on the basis of potency and act, cannot be understood entirely in those terms because the philosophy of being, as presented in Aristotle and Aquinas, does not as such disclose the fullness of ethical experience. It provides only what Wojtyła elsewhere calls the "metaphysical terrain" in which that experience moves ('Subjectivity and the Irreducible in the Human Being,' *PC:* 212-13). The full disclosure would be the disclosure of human subjectivity, the disclosure of the human "I" which is the subject and object, and indeed causal agent, of ethical experience. To achieve this disclosure Wojtyła considers it necessary, as has already been pointed out, to call upon the philosophy of consciousness as developed by the methods of phenomenology. But there is no realized phenomenology of the human person that Wojtyła thinks he can call upon. Such a phenomenology would be found in Scheler if it could be found anywhere, and it cannot be found in Scheler. For Scheler missed the decisive fact of agency. Wojtyła, then, by the very dialectic, as it were, of his own research and reflection, is forced to invent or construct a phenomenology of his own—the phenomenology of human agency. In fact he is forced to combine the reality of substance and act from the traditional philosophy of being with the subjectivity of the personal self from the modern philosophy of consciousness. One of them alone will not do. He has to have them both, and he has to have them both *together*, that is, as combined into a creative and mutually reinforcing unity. He has to have, in other words, the phenomenology of agency on the basis of the human suppositum. He has to have the phenomenology of the *acting person*.

3

The Acting Person

The Phenomenon of 'I Act'

"In its basic conception the whole of *The Acting Person* is grounded on the premise that *operari sequitur esse*" ('The Person: Subject and Community,' *PC:* 260 n6). This scholastic adage quoted by Wojtyła is usually taken in its metaphysical sense to refer to the fact that the activity of a thing (*operari*) depends on and follows the being or existence of that thing (*esse*), or that a thing acts according to the way it is. Wojtyła takes it, by contrast, in its epistemological sense. For if, he says, a thing's acting does depend on its being then, by the same token, a thing's acting must be the way to *know* its being, or the way it acts must be the clue to understanding the way it is. That, at any rate, is the assumption on which Wojtyła's major philosophical work *The Acting Person* proceeds. *Operari*, or what he calls the whole dynamism of the human being, is going to be how he seeks to understand the subjectivity of the human being. In phenomenological terms this means that he is going to investigate the phenomenon, the experienced reality, of "man acts" or "I act." For this phenomenon is how *operari* manifests itself to us in our lived experience of ourselves (*AP:* 9, 60).

What this experience is and discloses forms, argues Wojtyła, an integral whole. It can be analyzed into its aspects but these aspects are only parts of the whole and not the whole itself. Nevertheless they cannot be grasped all at once and need to be explicated progressively or one by one. The first part of the analysis concerns what one might call

23

the "I" of the "I act", or the aspect of consciousness in the acting person (*AP:* 28).

If a subject is to be an I it must somehow reflect back on itself and grasp this self as its own self, as both what it grasps and as what does that very grasping. There thus has to be both a sort of distance—I must become an object for myself—and a sort of identity—I must be the I that becomes an object for me. Wojtyła gives what amounts to a threefold analysis of this structure. There is first the fact of self-knowledge or the fact that, in addition to cognizing external things, we also cognize our own being and our own acts. Such self-knowledge is genuine cognition and, as such, it has the intentional structure of all cognitive acts. It intends an object that is transcendent to itself. The transcendent and intentional character of such self-cognition is what reveals and guarantees the objective existence of the self, or the fact that it is a real being in the world and not merely something constituted in and by consciousness (for otherwise we would be back in the error of subjectivism; *AP:* 33-34, 58-59).

Consciousness, however, is different from cognition (including self-cognition). It does not have an intentional or an objectifying character. It has rather two other functions, those of mirroring and reflexivity. These are the second and third parts of Wojtyła's analysis. As regards the mirroring function, this, as its name implies, is the function of immediately copying or reflecting all the acts and experiences that the self does and undergoes. Consciousness accompanies every act and experience and reproduces them, not indeed by re-performing them (that would be to do the act and have the experience all over again), but by keeping them alive for awareness. For it is clear that we do not just perform actions or undergo experiences; we are immediately aware that we are performing or undergoing them. We *accompany* ourselves, so to speak, as we perform and undergo. Such accompanying is the mirroring function of consciousness (*AP:* 31).

This mirroring gives us an inner view of our actions and experiences. It allows us to see that these actions and experiences, which by themselves are focused on their intended objects, are acts that proceed to those objects from within one's own self. But consciousness, to be complete, also has to perform the additional function of subjectivizing this inner view so that mirrored acts are experienced as my own. This is the reflexive function of consciousness. It is a natural and immediate turning back upon the subject so as to make the subject of the mirrored acts aware that it is the subject and that these acts are its own (*AP:* 31-48).

To put the point more briefly: self-cognition brings the self and the acts of the self to objective focus for the self (so that they are recognized as ontological realities); consciousness in its mirroring function keeps these acts, including self-cognition, present to the self or retains them in the self's own being, as it were; and consciousness in its reflexive function brings to light for the self that it is this very self.

Perhaps we should add about this analysis of how an I can be an I two things. First the analysis is not so much a proof as a description. The fact that the I is an I is a given of experience and does not need proof. It only needs explication. Second, because of the mirroring that is intrinsic to an I's being an I, everything that the I does or undergoes becomes for the I part of what the I is. It serves to constitute the I as this I, this unique and unrepeatable individual. It does not, to be sure, create the I, for the I is, in its metaphysical reality, a concrete suppositum from the beginning. But it does form and fashion this suppositum from within. It does make us to be the persons that, through the various stages of our lives, we progressively become. This I and this experience of the I are fundamental to the whole of Wojtyła's analysis of the person and of acting. For the analysis is made altogether from within the person, as it were, and rests for its evidence and its truth on the immediate experience persons have of themselves as "I".

The next step to note is that the experience of the I that Wojtyła takes as decisive for the person is the I of "I act." Here we are brought back to the theme of efficacy discussed in the previous chapter. "I act" or "man acts" is a matter of a subject, a self-conscious subject, causally producing an action. "I act" means that it is I that is the actor and doing the act, and not some other subject or actor. The acting is the I's own, and what this means is not only that the I has brought about the action but that, in bringing the action about, it has also brought itself about as cause and agent of the act. It has caused itself to be an actor. In this sense "I act" is different from "something happens in man". For while, in this latter case, a man is realized in some way or has some part of his dynamism activated (something really comes about in him), he is only realized as a subject. He is not also realized as the agent of what happens. Feelings, psychosomatic functionings, and so forth happen in man but man does not act in them. In the "I act," by contrast, man directly realizes himself and directly brings himself to activation. He is the "conscious cause of his own causation" (*AP:* 66). What this means is that in the moment and experience of efficacy there is both a certain transcendence and a certain immanence of man in his acting. He transcends himself in going beyond himself and in bringing about and sustaining in being some real effect; but he also remains in himself in the activation of himself that is precisely his bringing that effect about (*AP:* 61-71).

This acting of man, then, is his realizing of himself by himself. It proceeds from him and comes about in him because of his own agency. Here we come to the unity of the "I act," the unity of the "I" and the "act" taken together. For this fact of agency, the fact that in acting it is I who bring about the act and not something else outside my I, is at the center of the total experience of "I act." It contrasts sharply in this regard with the experience of "something happens in me." What happens in the self comes to the self regardless of the self and at times even despite the self. But what the self does comes out of the self's own activity and cannot happen regardless of or despite the self. Because of this, because the act is the self's own and is experienced as such, the act is also experienced as something that the self or the I *may* but *need not* do. It is experienced as an exercise of the self's freedom. For the self in acting is a self-moving agent or a self-causing cause and it is proper to such an agent or cause to act when and as it determines and not when and as something else determines. The I that acts in "I act" is a free self-determining I (*AP:* 96-101). Accordingly Wojtyła's analysis of "I act," taken in its totality, proceeds as an analysis of the self's free self-determination.

The Personal Structure of Self-Determination

It is we, then, who, insofar as we can be said to act at all, determine our acts and determine ourselves in our acts. This implies, first of all, the fact of *self-possession.* We cannot determine what we do not possess or what is not within our power to determine. Such self-possession was already integral to the self-consciousness discussed earlier; our knowing ourselves is also our possessing ourselves. But such self-possession appears more profoundly and more clearly in our self-determined activity. Also similarly apparent there, as an equal and co-constitutive factor, is the idea of *self-governance.* To determine oneself is to exercise governing control over oneself and over what one does and not to be governed in these respects by another. Such self-governance and self-possession necessarily involve the fact that the person is both subject and object of his action: I as subject possess and govern myself as object. This complex self-reflexive structure, whereby in acting (as also in knowing) the self turns back inwardly on itself in possession and rule of itself, contains in it a number of important elements and implications that reach through the whole of Wojtyła's reflections on the person. Self-determination is, in a way, the most pregnant of his phenomenological elaborations.

The first of these elements, already mentioned, is the idea of transcendence. In the self-determination of the "I act" the person is transcendent in his acting. This transcendence is in fact twofold: horizontal and vertical. Horizontal transcendence refers to the intentionality of "I will," that in acting the will intends an object beyond itself, some good or value, that it pursues. This horizontal transcendence is what is to the fore in the traditional, metaphysical analysis of willing which views willing primarily as some desiring or appetite of something. And this is not false, for there is such an object to the act of will. Moreover this transcendence is concerned with the good and bad, with moral values, in what is willed. This fact is picked up by Wojtyła in his more properly ethical reflections. But for the present, and for the understanding of the person, vertical transcendence is more important. This latter kind of transcendence was mentioned earlier as man's immanence, and it is what most of all must be attributed to the person in self-determination. The person has to transcend himself, or stand above himself, to determine himself, and this transcendence is immanent to the action in the sense that it is (partially) constitutive of action. Action here, or the determination of the will to this or that, is itself dependent on the decision of the self. Decision manifests the element of freedom in willing. For no object of the will, or nothing that belongs to horizontal transcendence, determines the action. The self has to decide and determine itself through its vertical transcendence. Decision is the constitutive element of "I will." Decision presupposes, of course, that there are things to decide about, and these are the values presented to the will fundamentally by cognition. But cognition is not enough. The will has to respond to the values cognized, and this response is not compelled. The person remains free with respect to objects of the will and is not determined but determines himself in the choice of one over another (*AP:* 105-35, 152).

The points that Wojtyła is making here are not, to be sure, original. One can find them already in different forms in other philosophers who thematized human action and human freedom. If there is any novelty here it is in the way Wojtyła reaches these points. For he reaches them, not from the metaphysical analysis of will (that it is a power directed to the universal good and so cannot be compelled by any particular good), but from the inner experience of the acting I, the phenomenology, of our own acts of willing and acting. The evidence of freedom and of its structure is here discovered in the givenness of our own everyday experience. This experience needs, of course, to be focused on if the evidence of freedom is to become clear, but there is no need for more than the experience. Moreover, to reject the experience and deny freedom in the name, say, of deterministic and materialistic science could only be the result of some narrowing down of experience according to preconceived, and not empirical, notions about matter. The experience must be allowed to speak for itself and right to the end, without prejudice (*AP:* 133). That is what the phenomenological method requires and what, indeed, gives it its strength.

A particular illustration of this can be found in something of special importance that comes out of that same phenomenological method. I refer to the inner structural connection that Wojtyła finds within consciousness between freedom and truth. Again, this view that there is such a connection is not new, but it does take on a new force, especially in the context of certain widespread contemporary opinions to the opposite effect. For the will, in choosing, focuses on some object of choice, something the I directly experiences as what it *may* choose but *need not* choose. Choice is not an arbitrary shooting in the dark. It is a deliberate selecting. Truth, says Wojtyła, is what releases the will from determination by the object and enables the person precisely to be self-determining in his acts with respect to all possible objects. The truth in question is in part the fact that the objects presented to choice are presented through cognition, and cognition is itself focused on truth, on the reality of what things are. Objects of choice thus do not come to me as forces or impulses that push me into action, as it were (for that would be to bypass the will and to make my choice to be determined by the object and not to be self-determined by me); they come to me as things with a determinate known value that can be compared with other things according to that same known value. Truth, the cognized truth of the object, mediates the object and the will so that values do not compel but are freely responded to by the will. For it is not just that cognition knows truth; it is also the case that will responds to truth. Will itself, in its own structure, is referred to the truth and wants the truth in what it wills. The will wants true goods, not things that appear to be good and are not. There is a specific moment of "surrender to truth" already in volition before any object is presented to it for choice. The orientation to truth, in other words, is constitutive of the will and of the will's power of self-determination. The two together—truth in cognition and the intrinsic orientation to truth in the will—are what make freedom and choice possible.

Of course, this is not to say that we always do cognize truth or that we always respond to the truth when we cognize it. We can err in judgment and we can choose against the truth of the good. Intellectual error and bad choice are facts manifest to experience, and defects manifest to experience too. A striking sign of this is the experience of sin and guilt which are not merely error and the consciousness of error in judgment (such error could be involuntary); they are also error and the consciousness of error in choice (such error has to be voluntary because it is internal to the choosing). But there cannot be error, or any consciousness of error, without a truth by which to judge error and, moreover, without an intrinsic ordination to and desire for truth in cognition and choice. Erroneous choice would not be sin and would not lead to guilt if error were not somehow a defect, a distortion, within the structure of choice itself and were not experienced as such. The phenomenon of choosing, of self-determination, and of guilt and sin and their opposites, are direct personal experiences of the inherence of truth in the structure of "I act" (*AP:* 135-43).

Fulfillment, Duty, Conscience, Responsibility, Felicity

There are other elements in the structure of "I act" that are contained in the moment of truth in choice and manifest themselves in the experience of choice. They include fulfillment, conscience, duty, responsibility, and felicity.

One of the features of any act of the person is that it is a realization of the dynamism (the power to act and to be) of the person. As already noted, in performing an act man himself becomes an actor and activates his being insofar as he acts. Every act is therefore a fulfillment of his being (which is further evidence of the ontological reality of man—a pure consciousness, made up of a stream of actual states of consciousness, could not become fulfilled; only a real suppositum with real potentialities could do that; *AP:* 153-54). But because of truth, which is integral to free action, this fulfillment takes on a twofold modality: it can be either good or bad depending on whether the object chosen is a true good or not. Moral good and bad are a real part of the experience of "I act," as is manifest in that experience

29

itself. Strictly speaking, however, only in good acts is there fulfillment proper, for only such acts realize the person according to what the person is, that is, according to the orientation to the truth that is intrinsic to the structure of self-determination. Evil or bad bring nonfulfillment. Still even this nonfulfillment is a becoming of the person. Hence in the doing of good and bad the person himself becomes good or bad. The good or bad act may, as an actual performance, come and go quickly. But it remains in the person through the vertical transcendence of self-determination whereby the acting is taken up into, and helps constitute, the self or the I that the person is continually becoming (*AP:* 149-52).

Here also is where duty and conscience become manifest. The sense of duty is "the experiential form of the reference to (or dependence on) the moral truth" (*AP:* 156). It is related also to the idea of norms. A norm expresses the truth about the good, but it addresses this truth to the will and takes hold of the dynamism of the will, or its power to act, in the form of a command or prohibition ('Human Nature as the Basis of Ethical Formation,' *PC:* 98). The positing of norms belongs to the lived experience of the truth of the good, which positing is not just a matter of determining the truth about the goodness of a proposed human action but also a matter of directing action in keeping with the truth ('On the Metaphysical and Phenomenological Basis of the Moral Norm,' *PC:* 91, 93). Norms have, as Wojtyła puts it, a dynamic character. They call on the will to act or not to act according to the truth of the good. Wojtyła here brings an element of Kantianism into his reflections and supplements the idea of objective value (from Scheler) with that of a sense of duty (from Kant). Wojtyła does nevertheless reject the Kantian idea of a pure duty unrelated to cognized goods. In this he follows Scheler, and indeed Aquinas, both of whom trace "ought" or obligation to the truth of the good. But Wojtyła very much insists against Scheler, but with Aquinas, that morality does contain the idea of duty and norms. For it is very much part of the lived experience of morality that one should respond appropriately to the truth of the good. Such is the role of conscience where is achieved that union of moral truthfulness and duty that manifests itself in the normative power of the good. "In each of his actions the human person is eyewitness of the transition from the 'is' to the 'should'—the transition from 'X is truly good' to 'I should do X'" (*AP:* 162). The truth of the good becomes, we may say, the obligation to pursue this truth through the fact of the will's freedom or through the fact that the will, precisely as such, is referred to the truth of the good. Hence to experience the truth of the good is to experience the duty of the good too. And that is conscience.

The experience of guilt can be particularly illuminating here. Guilt not only includes the idea of a norm but highlights the dynamic character of norms. The experience of guilt is the experience of acting, not against a good or value merely, but against a norm, a principle of good and evil, whose obligatory force one also recognizes. Man's fulfillment, therefore, is achieved through his sense of obligation, his sense of the call of the truth in good, as the peculiar modification of his self-determination and intentionality ('The Problem of the Theory of Morality,' *PC:* 136-39; *AP:* 169). At the same time man too is engaged as himself a value. Any intentional act of the will toward value is also an act intransitive in the agent and remains in and turns back on the agent. Hence the basic value of the person as the subject of the will and as the agent of actions is also engaged. Man is an object, an internal object, of his own actions. This is clearly built into the idea of fulfillment. It is a fact whose significance, as we shall see in the next chapter, is brought to the fore in Wojtyła's elaboration of what he calls "the personalistic norm."

Wojtyła stresses that this recognition of and response to the truth of the good that is internal to the act of the person supports neither Kantian autonomy (the view that conscience makes its own laws) nor the externalism of a mechanical deduction of norms from abstract formulas. Conscience discovers norms; it does not create them (that would lead to arbitrary individualism). But these norms are not external and alien to conscience. On the contrary, because of the moment of truth, conscience, which is ordered to truth, recognizes these norms as in a sense its own. Truth does not abolish freedom; it "liberates" freedom. Truth "relieves the tension" that would otherwise exist between "the objective order of norms" and the "inner freedom" of the person (*AP:* 166). This tension is intensified, on the other hand, by mere external compulsion and command. But once the norms are acknowledged as true by conscience, they are no longer external. They become internal and form and create personal freedom. The hostile pressure of rules forcibly imposed is dissolved when these rules are seen by the self through conscience as true and good. A set of objective moral norms, in other words, far from being (as is often alleged) opposed to the person and the person's freedom, is, as founded on the truthfulness of conscience towards the good, the very possibility of freedom (*AP:* 152-69).

Man's efficacy in acting, the fact that it is he who is the cause of the act, also leads to the idea of responsibility. If it is I who act then it is I who am responsible for the act. And I am responsible in two basic ways. First of all I am responsible for the truthfulness of the act, for the fact that the act does correspond to the true value of the object of the act. If my act, for instance, has another person as object then the act must correspond to the value of the person. This fact of truthfulness reveals, as will be discussed later, the natural law character of Wojtyła's ethics (that acts are right when they accord with the nature of their object as determinative of the true value of the object). Second, I am, in acting, responsible to myself. The act is mine and its truthfulness or lack thereof is also mine. Conscience judges this truthfulness and so stands as judge over my acting—condemning if the action is not truthful and approving if it is. Thus, just as a person is the one who governs and is governed by himself, and just as he is the one who possesses and is possessed by himself, so also is he the one who answers to himself in responsibility for himself. His actions are his own and as his own he judges them. This fact brings home even more how much truth and norms and law in the moral life are internal to the person and belong to his very structure as agent. They do not exist merely as external to him—though they are objectively right and though he does not create them. Their objective rightness is something that is internalized in the subject's own dynamic structure and has to be so internalized if truth, norms, and law are to be determinative for his acting. It is in this way that Wojtyła dissolves the autonomy/ heteronomy split and the subjective/objective split in ethical thinking. Properly understood the two terms in each split are one; indeed they have to be one if the "I act" of the person is to make sense. The person needs objectivity to be a responsible subject, and he needs the objectivity of moral norms to be a self-determining agent. The person, in other words, needs truth to be free, to be the self-determining subject that he really is. Or, in short, he needs truth to be himself (*AP:* 169-74).

The person also needs truth to be happy or to achieve felicity. Felicity here means fulfillment. One is happy and achieves felicity through being fulfilled. This fulfillment, however, is precisely what has just been discussed, namely acting out the truth in freedom or, as Wojtyła himself calls it, "the fulfillment of freedom through truth" (*AP:* 175). Felicity, therefore, is something internal to the good act and is part of its structure, part of the vertical transcendence that makes action a distinctive becoming or realizing of the agent. That realizing, if it is good, is fulfillment and therewith felicity. That is why happiness cannot be identified with pleasure or indeed with consequences.

Pleasure belongs more to what happens in man than to what man does; felicity should rather be called joy than pleasure. By the same token happiness is not the consequences of the act, whether for oneself or others, since these are external to the acting and to the fulfillment that the acting is. Hedonism and utilitarianism, therefore, are wholly inadequate understandings whether of moral goodness or of happiness (*AP:* 174-78).

The Integration of the Person in the Action

The transcendence of the person in acting, the fact that he stands above himself and determines himself in the way discussed, is not all that concerns the phenomenon of "I act." There is also the fact of integration. Self-possession and self-governance (the parts that make up the structure of self-determination) require not only that the self governs and possesses but also that it is possessed and governed. This subjectiveness of man, the fact that he is the subject as well as the agent of action, needs to be fully thematized too. Of course, this was, in a way, already done in Wojtyła's analysis of self-determination (for that includes both the agent and the subject sides of action). But there is need to take the analysis further. For in the subject man there are, as is manifest, physical and emotional elements too and these need to be given their place in the structure of self-determination. Evidence for this comes from the phenomena of disintegration, where man's subjectivity is precisely not integrated (physical disabilities, neuroses, instinctive and emotive disorders), and where the person suffers an inability, more or less severe, to govern and possess himself. Integration, then, concerns the parts of the person's subjectivity which, taken by themselves, are extrinsic to self-determination, and thus primarily his bodily and emotional powers. These have a dynamism of their own, but if that dynamism is to be made personal it must be brought within the scope of, and subordinated to, the structure of self-determination. This is what is meant by integration and only in integration do these powers take on the meaning and quality proper to personal existence. Taken in abstraction, as they are when studied in the particular sciences, they lack this meaning. The sciences may be able to provide material for the understanding of the person but by themselves they do not reach that level and do not reveal the personal reality of man's somatic and psychic operations. The person-action unity in the "I act," as it has so far been analyzed, is logically prior to the psychosomatic unity. Hence, in the analysis of the person, it must take precedence. Accordingly Wojtyła studies these operations from within that perspective, the perspective of integration (*AP:* 196-200, 220).

'Soma' in Wojtyła's analysis does not precisely mean body nor does 'psyche' precisely mean soul. Soma is more properly the bodily functions as they enter into lived experience, and the psyche is more properly the feelings and emotions as they also enter into it. These aspects of experience were earlier identified as what happens in man in contrast to what man does. But integration introduces these "happenings" into "doing" and makes them play an active part there. They thus belong to man not simply as he is a suppositum or ontic reality (the suppositum, recall, is the ontological locus of everything that is in man, whether active or passive, potential or actual), but also as he is an agent. They come to have a place in man's efficacy and not just in his subjectivity. In this regard what is distinctive of the soma, on the one hand, is "reactivity," which refers to the body both as it is outwardly discernible (limbs, shape, and so forth), and also as it is experienced from within in its organic functioning (muscle movements, heart beats, and so forth). What is distinctive of the psyche, on the other hand, is those functions (like perceiving, feeling, emotions) which are not as such corporeal but do depend on the body (fear is not, as such, the quick beating of the heart even if it involves it). The integration of the person in the action rests on the psychic and the somatic as a mutually conditioning and dynamic totality (*AP:* 199, 202).

The body or the soma (to take this first) is the territory and means for the performance of action and for the fulfillment of the person. It is also what places man in the realm of nature, making him share the external conditions of existence alongside the other animals. The vitalities of the body are primarily vegetative and reproductive and these, as such, are instinctive and spontaneous and not dependent on the self-determination of the person (digestion and gestation, for instance, just happen, regardless of what we may wish, after our acts of eating or copulating). Such things also generally escape man's consciousness and are not mirrored or taken up into his self-awareness. They operate, or fail to operate, on their own. Still, they are related to man's subjectivity and make possible the acts of the body that are under the control of self-determination. It is thus, for instance, that physical skills can be developed in the body. Of course the body can fail here and disease and loss of limbs can limit what a man can do. But these defects have a merely somatic and not a moral significance. Someone who is disabled is not thereby distorted in what makes him a person, for somatic disabilities remain external to the person. "A human being with a high degree of somatic disintegration may represent a personality of great value" (*AP:* 215). The disabled, therefore, whether physically or mentally so, remain fully persons and retain all the value that belongs to persons (the value inherent in the structure of transcendence). There can be no case for setting them on a lower level or of making them instruments to others' goals and interests.

The body is also the ground or basis for certain instincts, as those of self-preservation and reproduction. But these instincts are not purely somatic, though they are rooted in the body. They also enter into the psychic and emotional life of man and thereby also into his self-determination. For that reason the significance of these instincts is not first in the bodily reactions but in the objective values and ends towards which they point—for that is the sphere of the self-determination of the person. Here we find anticipations of Wojtyła's moral positions, that sexual activity is not a matter of instinct but of the true values present in the objective nature of the sexual act. Man is determined by himself in the recognition of truth, not by instincts or reactions unrelated to truth (*AP:* 215-19).

By the psyche Wojtyła means emotivity, and by that he means the complex of feelings, emotions, sensations, and related behaviors and attitudes, or all those things that have some dependence on the body (feelings and emotions have bodily occasions and correlates) but are not identical with it (emotions, for instance, are not vegetative reactions like digestion). One special feature of emotivity is that it contains a sensitivity to values. The emotions are sensitive responses to good and evil, and they can serve to intensify and heighten one's awareness of good and evil, rendering them vivid in a way that consciousness alone does not do. But emotive responses to values are not yet truthfulness about values. They are only raw material, as it were, for the will and need to be integrated into the person through truthfulness. It is such integration that is decisive for the acting person. Indeed the moment of truthfulness here is so important that self-determination may require one to act without or even against feelings. To follow feelings alone would be to lose oneself in what "happens" and become incapable of self-determination. Still, the emotions have their special role in accompanying the moral dimensions of self-determination, as in the case of the remorse and distress that accompany guilt and in the peace and joy that accompany repentance or justification or conversion. Emotions also have a rich and complex diversification—joy, sorrow, anger, tenderness, love, hatred—and a difference of modality—being excitable or stirring, deep or peripheral—that to some extent defies complete classification (*AP:* 220-42).

Emotions are things that happen in man as their subject, often spontaneously. Also, because of the intense way they can affect us, they present a special task for self-determination and self-governance to cope with. It can be difficult to integrate them into the self. Nevertheless emotions are not, as such, a disintegrating force. They are rather material for integration and a part of the subjectivity of man that needs to be synthesized with his efficacy. This synthesis can require effort and it can fail. Emotion can take over from the will and freedom in the determination of action and can lead to subjectivism, the dominance of subjectivity over efficacy. In extreme cases there can be a loss of responsibility, whether partial or even total, for what is done. But efficacy and emotion should go together, and emotions, with all their richness and vividness, should enhance the experience of value and the exercise of self-determination. The person in his acting should be an actor, but a full-blooded actor (if I may so speak). He must be an integrated unity.

Man's emotional dynamism, in fact, introduces into man its own spontaneous turn to values, whether of an attractive or repulsive sort. This spontaneity must, however, be integrated with and into the discernment of the truth about good and evil. This is where the moral virtues come in, which are a sort of proficiency in integration. They make the best use of emotive energy rather than suppress it and in fact take over this energy for enhancing the energy of the will. For, as this integration with truth and self-determination progresses, emotions in their spontaneous moves of attraction and repulsion become sources for a spontaneous movement of the will itself toward real good and away from real bad. Perfecting this integration is a task for a lifetime, but it is part of the general realization of the personal structure of self-governance and self-possession in the complex unity that is man (*AP:* 253).

The integration of the person in action, and even more the transcendence of the person in action, reveal the spiritual nature of man, the fact that there is in him a factor that is inherently irreducible to matter. For the person stands above himself, as it were, in his self-determination and exercises a certain superiority over himself (this is his vertical transcendence, of course, which is, after all, a sort of self-transcendence). At the same time the person is the one who is thus subordinate to himself. He is both the superior and the subordinate; he is both transcendent and integrated, and integrated precisely into the transcendence. This superiority is the essence of his spirituality, his irreducibility to matter (something wholly material could not transcend itself in action, could not surrender to truth, and could not freely determine itself). Yet this spirituality penetrates into the person's materiality, his soma and his psyche, integrating them into the spirituality. Something purely material could not spiritualize the material like this. The spiritual factor is thus the integrating and unifying element in man. It points to the soul and, in a way, is already an indirect experience of the soul. However, a full analysis of the being of the soul belongs, says Wojtyła, to the philosophy of being. It is enough for him now to have shown, from within the philosophy of consciousness, the fundamental immateriality of the human person (*AP:* 179-86, 255-58).

Participation

The analyses discussed so far cover most of *The Acting Person* and more or less complete the phenomenology of the acting person as that concerns the person in his acts as such. These analyses form the basis for everything that Wojtyła has to say about ethics, and they transfer into his theology too. They have, however, within *The Acting Person* an immediate application to the understanding of persons in their acting together, or what Wojtyła calls "participation." This understanding itself already has some ethical and political implications that it is necessary to draw out. They will lead the way into Wojtyła's expressly ethical reflections in *Love and Responsibility*. Nevertheless, the focus of the discussion of participation is still on the structure of the person in the phenomenon "I act," and on the consequences for this structure that follow from the fact that acting together with others is a universal phenomenon among human beings. The ethical and political implications, however, are in this case much closer to the surface.

The first point to note or recall is that the action of the person has a personalistic value before and in addition to any moral value it may also have. Moral values inhere in the action, of course, because of the moment of truth present in human action. For the personal structure of self-determination includes in it a necessary reference to truth and the good is normative for action through the mediation of truth about the good. The personalistic value, by contrast, is simply the fact that man does act as a man (and not by mere instinct or impulse), that he performs an action according to the requirements of self-determination and realizes transcendence and integration in their several stages. It is in this personalistic value, in fact, that is found the most fundamental manifestation of the worth of the person (this worth of the person becomes, as we shall see in the next chapter, the basis of the personalistic norm).

The relation between the personalistic value and the moral value of an act rests on the fact that, unless an act is genuinely performed (unless an act is a genuine case of self-determination), there can be no question of whether it is morally good or bad. Where self-determination is lacking or diminished there is no or a diminished responsibility, and no or a diminished merit or demerit can be attributed to the man and to the act. Still, the moral value of the act is not simply the same as the fact that the act was authentically performed, or was an authentic act. Rather, the moral value presupposes this and rests on it. This remains true even though a morally bad act betokens also some diminution of the personalistic structure of "I act," the diminution involved in its being a denial, or rejection, of the moment of truthfulness to good and bad. Moral good and bad belong to the act because of the reference to a norm about the truth of the good and bad and the corresponding summons to act on that truth. One can, however, prescind from this reference to a norm and consider the act, and the moment of truth, only as they are internal to the act. The personalistic value thus inheres in the very performance itself of the action, in the very fact that man acts, while the moral value comes to the act because of the additional reference to a norm (*AP:* 264-63).

Now man is manifestly a social animal who acts together with other men in a multitude of ways. This acting together, if it is to be authentic action, must somehow be fitted into the structure of self-determination that constitutes human action. This is where participation properly comes in. For the main idea of participation is that in his acting with others a man should be able to, and should in fact, retain the personalistic value of his own action. His acting with others should be both a sharing in the realization and results of this acting together and, at the same time, should be his own acting and should really be an actualizing of his own self-determination.

> It is the person's transcendence in the action when the action
> is being performed "together with others"—transcendence
> which manifests that the person...stands out as having
> retained his very own freedom of choice and direction—which
> is the basis as well as the condition of participation...To be
> capable of participation thus indicates that man, when he acts

together with other men, retains in this acting the personalistic value of his own action and at the same time shares in the realization and the results of communal acting (*AP:* 269).

What this means is, first, that a man chooses what is also chosen by others and, second, that he chooses it fully and authentically as something he can and does make his own. If this is not the case there is no genuine participation and, in a way, no genuine acting. Or at least there is no genuine acting as far as that person is concerned who does not participate. What is lost here is, of course, the personalistic value of the act quite independently of any moral value involved. So, if human community is the acting together of those who make up the community, there must be an obligation to make participation possible; and human community, in order to be a community in acting, should be conducted with this object in view. Directly from the personalistic value of acting, therefore, it follows that the person has the natural right, and obligation, precisely as a person, to perform actions, communal or otherwise, and to be fulfilled in them. At any rate the existence of such a right and obligation must follow from what it is to be a person, and from what it is to act together, if truthfulness to the person and to action is to be observed in one's actions (*AP:* 267-71, 323-27). This is, in fact, an immediate application of the personalistic norm, the norm to respect the person as what he is, which will be discussed in more detail in the next chapter.

As instances of failure in this regard Wojtyła gives the extremes of what he calls individualism and totalism. The first of these arises from a lack in the person who is the subject and agent of the acting, and the second arises from defects in the way the community of acting operates. The first subordinates the community to the individual and the second subordinates the individual to the community.

In the first, acting with others is viewed as a limitation and even as an impediment to the agent's own realization. It gets in the way of what he wants. The purpose of the community in such a case is then reduced to protecting the good of the individual from being interfered with by others. But this, of course, amounts to the denial of real acting together. It makes any genuine participation impossible when it comes to matters of common concern. Such matters get accomplished, no doubt, but not communally; they are imposed by "the authorities" and are accepted as necessary evils, not as anything positive for the individual as such. Wojtyła does not specify which if any actual communities or societies this picture represents but it would be hard not to recognize elements of it in theories of contemporary liberal democracy and in Hobbesian theories of politics. The opposite system of totalism or, as Wojtyła also calls it, reversed individualism, is characterized by the need to find protection for the community from the individual. The individual is seen as an enemy of the common good (just as, in the other case, the common good is seen as an enemy, a limitation, of the individual). The reason is that totalism, like individualism, sees the individual as focused on individual goods alone and hence concludes that a common good can only be pursued by setting limits on the individual. This usually means a considerable amount of sheer coercion. It certainly means that the individual is prevented from choosing the good from within his own freedom according to the principles of genuine participation. Again Wojtyła does not specify which societies are totalist, but it would be hard not to see in totalism the system produced by communism and socialism, the system under which Wojtyła spent most of his adult years.

The view of man that underlies both these systems is anti-personalistic insofar as neither recognizes participation as appropriate to the person or as part of his authentic self-determination and fulfillment as a person. If a system is to be personalistic it must give persons "freedom in the action" so that they can fulfill themselves in the free performance of what they do. On the basis of such personalism it follows, according to Wojtyła, that man has the right, even within community, to total freedom of acting. But this does not mean that he may do what he likes and without regard for moral values, or for the normativity of the truth of the good. Moral values are not opposed to the personalistic value since only in choosing what is morally good does man fulfill himself and realize his freedom, his power of self-determination. Man therefore has total freedom of action, but this freedom is not an unattached absolute. It is conditioned, and conditioned from within, by the moral good and by the truth about the good. Man may have the right to free action but he does not have the right to do wrong. Indeed such a right would, in the end, destroy freedom (*AP*: 271-76, 328-32).

What is lacking in these systems is "community," which Wojtyła uses as a term to express the reality of participation, of acting and existing with others. For as participation, or the capacity for it, is a property of the person (the human person is a social being), so it is a constitutive factor of the community. Person and community, therefore, naturally go together and coalesce. They are not alien or mutually opposed to each other as individualism and totalism suppose. The community is, nevertheless, not itself a kind of real subject. It has only a "quasi subjectiveness." What Wojtyła means by this is that the only proper subjects are individual persons. Only they are real supposita and self-determining causes of action. The community is not a new person or suppositum alongside individual persons. It is not a hypostatized subject. It belongs, rather, to the accidental order and is a matter of new relations existing among real subjects, real acting persons. Wojtyła instances the relations of kinship, being a compatriot, being a citizen, and being a member of a religious group. These new relations are founded on some notion of a common good. The common good is the real, objective good of the community. But, for a community to exist, that good has to be chosen by each of the members of the community. This choosing is not just a matter of making that good their own good through an authentic act of self-determination. It is also a matter of choosing the same good as others choose and of choosing it because they choose it. Both the objective moment—the good of communal living and its conditions—and the subjective moment—the participation of each through the exercise of free choice—are required for genuine community.

Wojtyła sees two attitudes that are proper to community, those of solidarity and opposition. Solidarity indicates a constant readiness to accept and realize one's share in community and to do so in view of the benefit of the whole. This involves, in particular, what Wojtyła calls complementarity, which is a refraining to take over the part of others or to trespass upon others' duties (unless, of course, the common good, together with one's basic solidarity towards the common good, require it). Opposition is when, in the name of genuine participation, one opposes what is, or what one judges to be, contrary to the common good. Opposition is thus integral to solidarity. Wojtyła instances as examples of opposition parents disagreeing about the education of children or politicians about the welfare of the nation or state. These can, and would ordinarily, be instances of solidarity because of the deep concern of both parties for the common good. They are also, and for the same reason, in principle constructive. One can say, indeed, that the structure of human community is correct if it allows for the presence and effectiveness of a just opposition. Here is where Wojtyła introduces the further element of dialogue, of the frank exchange of different opinions about the good and what the good requires. Properly understood dialogue is the formation and strengthening of interhuman solidarity through the attitude of opposition. Of course, opposition and dialogue with opponents can also bring strains and difficulties. But they are not to be rejected, or suppressed, on that account. There can be something true in views opposed to the prevailing consensus, and if so the truth in these views should not be rejected but should, in the name of the human good, be taken up and integrated into the community (*AP:* 276-87, 332-44).

One might be tempted to see in Wojtyła's ideas of opposition and dialogue elements of the thought of John Stuart Mill and of more recent writers on democracy and democratic political theory who also stress the importance of allowing for, encouraging, and embracing differences of opinion in political life. But whatever might be true of these writers, one should remember in Wojtyła's case that he always stresses the fact that there is an objective truth to be had in ethics and politics and, moreover, that the moment of truth is an inseparable element of human freedom, without which it would not really be freedom. Wojtyła is no skeptic after the manner of Mill, nor does an appeal to skepticism play any role in his argument. On the contrary, to deny the possibility of objective truth and of knowledge when it comes to human action would be to destroy the very structure of human action. It would therefore be to destroy, not to guarantee or preserve, the possibility of opposition and dialogue as well as of solidarity and community generally.

In contrast, however, to these authentic attitudes of solidarity and opposition there are the inauthentic attitudes of conformism and noninvolvement or avoidance, where the personalistic value of action is lacking. We all have, to some extent, a natural tendency to conform, to comply with accepted customs, and this is as such something positive and creative. But it ceases to be so when it becomes servile and leads to a lack of solidarity and an avoidance of opposition. It then becomes conformism, or a mere outward conformity, because it ceases to be an authentic action and does not engage the person in his free self-determination. Such conformism consists in an attitude of compliance and resignation. In fact it falls back into the sphere of what merely happens in man. The person avoids seeking fulfillment of himself in acting along with others. Participation ceases. This not only harms the person involved (for he ceases to act and fulfill himself as a person) but also the community, for the common good is no longer cared for or promoted by true participation. There is (outward) uniformity but no (inward) unity.

Avoidance or noninvolvement is the inauthentic counterpart to opposition. It consists in a certain withdrawal and a lack of active concern for the common good. Indeed it borders, in a way, on conformism, for it amounts to a letting the community be without any effort to oppose it where it is going wrong. Wojtyła allows that there are occasions when people withdraw in the hope that their very absence might be more telling as an act of opposition than their active engagement would be. But absence can just as well be a kind of compensatory attitude for those who find solidarity too difficult and do not believe in opposing the status quo. To the extent, however, that there are reasons to justify such withdrawal, then these reasons must amount in themselves to an accusation of the community and a charge that it is seriously defective and that the common good has been compromised or falsely understood. For participation is a fundamental human good. It cannot rightly be refused unless the community one is withdrawing from has ceased to make genuine participation possible. At all events, noninvolvement without any such justification is, like conformism, an inauthentic attitude insofar as it deprives a man of the opportunity to perform actions and to fulfill himself authentically in action along with others (*AP:* 288-91, 344-48).

Wojtyła does no more than outline these points in *The Acting Person*. He admits that he does not develop them into a full-blown analysis or carry them over into a complete theory of politics. It is not hard, nevertheless, to see some of the broad outlines of how such a theory would go. Wojtyła himself has already implicitly noted (in his discussion of individualism and totalism) what sort of judgment must be passed on the two main modern systems of communism and liberal democracy. Neither is going to turn out to be satisfactory, whether in the way it is lived or in the way it understands itself, even if the latter is much less bad in these regards than the former. One can, however, easily extrapolate other elements of Wojtyła's implicit politics. The different behaviors of different people under harsh or restrictive regimes (or indeed under any regime where some are trying to use the forces of the state to exclude or marginalize people or groups of people and to push through their own personal agenda) will receive praise or blame as they manifest the several authentic or inauthentic attitudes just discussed. Certainly it will be relatively straightforward to work out, in the light of Wojtyła's analysis of participation, how to identify genuine cases of racism or sexism or religious persecution, for instance, and to say what is wrong with them. For all arrangements of community that exclude some of the members from participation (that is from exercising their freedom and realizing their fulfillment as persons in the life and deeds of the community) will be unjust precisely in those respects. The excluded will, therefore, have the right and the duty to protest and oppose the injustice. Conversely, the community will have the duty to allow that opposition and, with its aid, to admit the fault and seek out ways to set it right.

One should, therefore, notice the final part of Wojtyła's analysis of participation and therewith the final part of *The Acting Person*. Here he introduces the idea of "neighbor" as opposed to that of member of community. The idea of neighbor is based on the simple fact of our common humanness, that is to say, it is based on what is common to all men everywhere including myself, and not on what is common to these or those men who compose this or that community. As such the idea of neighbor is the fundamental basis of, and deeper than, all membership of particular communities. It forms, in a sense, the idea of the human community as such. Any of the more particular communities that detach themselves from this base of common humanity lose their properly human character and, in a way, cease to be communities at all. For in denying or relegating humanness they deny the dimension of participation that makes the community. Participation is first and foremost a human thing and cannot be realized if humanness is denied. The term 'neighbor' thus brings out, for Wojtyła, the full significance of participation. The ability to share in the humanness of every man is where participation reaches its personal depth and its universal dimension. It is also the core of participation and the condition for the personalistic value of acting along with others. It establishes and confirms the universality of human existence, or the fact that, despite all the particular differences that separate us from one another (historical, cultural, personal, and so forth), we all share in the one humanness and all achieve fulfillment through the same authentic dynamism of freedom and self-determination.

The idea of neighbor brings with it the commandment of love, the commandment to love one's neighbor as oneself. This commandment becomes the core principle of Wojtyła's ethics. Love of neighbor is, of course, an idea that found classic expression in the Gospels and Wojtyła is more than happy to recognize his indebtedness to them. However, abstracting from the more properly evangelical depth of that expression, we must recognize that the idea of love of neighbor has a philosophical and phenomenological foundation too. It is something that can be recognized from within our experience of the personhood of ourselves and others. It expresses a special attitude of regard that we should have towards every person simply because of the fact of their personhood. Every person should be treated as a person and not as a means for furthering one's own interests. Love of neighbor is in fact the necessary basis for any community that is to be human, and for any relation to a member of a particular community. Without it there arises the phenomenon of what Wojtyła calls alienation.

Alienation signifies that man is deprived of the personalistic value of his action. Such privation can, indeed, happen because of the system of things (the system of production and distribution of goods, the blind pursuit of progress, and so forth); but its root is deeper and more personal in man himself. For it is man who creates systems and who is therefore responsible for the alienation present in a system. The fundamental source of alienation is disregard of the command to love one's neighbors, one's fellow human beings, in all their fullness as persons. In order to overcome alienation love of neighbor must be at the foundation of all the communities and systems that man develops and establishes at any level. Alienation is only in the system because it is first in man, the acting person who embraces or fails to embrace, in his action, the true human good and genuine participation with others. Reform and correction must therefore be pursued in the same way. It must focus on man first and foremost, and on making love of neighbor the ultimate criterion in forming communities. Only secondarily may it focus on the system (*AP:* 292-99, 348-55).

4

Love and Responsibility

The Personalistic Norm

Wojtyła's other main philosophical work, *Love and Responsibility*, presents a striking and informative illustration of how the phenomenology of *The Acting Person* issues in definite ethical principles and practices. True, this book, as mentioned already in chapter one above, was written and published before *The Acting Person*. But it depends logically on some such philosophical anthropology as is found in *The Acting Person* and anyway, as a matter of fact, *The Acting Person* does help in decisive ways to illuminate the theses and the argument of *Love and Responsibility*. In addition *Love and Responsibility* begins by laying out certain theses about the person that anticipate, and also get deepened in, the analyses of *The Acting Person*.

Love and Responsibility, as its name in part indicates, is about responsible love between husband and wife. It is basically a book about the ethics of marriage. It does indeed touch on a good many other issues as it proceeds, but the focus is always on marriage. The book could, therefore, appear to be a rather narrow one, of relevance to the ethics of marriage but not of much relevance elsewhere. Such a judgment would be premature. The book may have a specific theme but the principles and analyses from which it proceeds have a universal relevance. They could, indeed, be applied almost directly to a host of other contentious ethical issues. That is why the book transcends, so to speak, its own limits as regards its significance for the understanding of Wojtyła's overall philosophical thought.

At all events the core of the book is a principle of ethics that has a virtually unlimited application. Wojtyła calls it the "Personalistic Norm." The book, in fact, begins with certain claims about the person that are central for establishing and formulating the norm. They are: that the person is an objective reality in the world, that he has a unique interior life that revolves around truth and goodness, that he possesses the power of free self-determination. All these theses, of course, recall and repeat what is said in *The Acting Person*—about man as a suppositum and about the moment of truth and about self-determination in the phenomenon of "I act." But in *Love and Responsibility* Wojtyła immediately proceeds to draw a conclusion left implicit in *The Acting Person* that is decisive for the formulation of the personalistic norm. It is the thesis that the person, as free, is his own master and judge and does not fall under the right or possession of another. As Wojtyła puts it:

> No one else can want for me. No one can substitute his act of will for mine. It does sometimes happen that someone very much wants me to want what he wants. This is the moment when the impassable frontier between him and me, which is drawn by free will, becomes most obvious. I may not want that which he wants me to want—and in this precisely I am *incommunicabilis* (not capable of transmission, not transferable). I am and I must be independent in my actions. All human relationships are posited on this fact. All true conceptions about education and culture begin from and return to this point (*LR:* 24, 21-23).

Such a thesis clearly recalls the teaching of *The Acting Person* from which, of course, it follows as a consequence. From it in turn follows, as another consequence, the ethical thesis that when one's actions have for object another person (as they do above all in the case of marriage and spousal love) they must accord with the facts about the person as just set out. So, for instance, it is contrary to the idea of the person to treat someone else as a means or an instrument for one's use or enjoyment. This would effectively subordinate the other person to one's own ends whereas, according to the above quotation and to the idea of free self-determination, each person has their own ends and must be treated as having their own ends (and not as having ends imposed on them willy nilly by someone else). This moral injunction and its precise meaning need further elaboration, which Wojtyła does proceed to give. But it is worth pointing out first that Wojtyła's reasoning here has a fundamentally natural law character.

Consider the following:

> [A] person must not be *merely* the means to an end for another person. This is precluded by the very nature of personhood, by what any person is. For a person is a thinking subject and capable of taking decisions: these, most notably, are the attributes we find in the inner self of the person. This being so, every person is by nature capable of determining his or her aims. Anyone who treats a person as the means to an end does violence to the very essence of the other, to what constitutes its natural right. Obviously we must demand from a person, as a thinking individual, that his or her ends should be genuinely good, since the pursuit of evil ends is contrary to the rational nature of the person (*LR*: 26-27).

One can ask about this argument, as about any argument that moves from an assertion about something to an injunction to behave in a certain way, how this move is actually made and justified. The basic answer is that the facts involved, the natures of the things in question, contain an evaluative dimension, so that goodness is already intrinsic to the fact. Natures themselves are goods and contain an implicit norm directed to reason and the will that they be treated accordingly (*LR*: 294 n20).

This point can perhaps be made more luminous if one connects it with the moment of truth inherent in freedom as analyzed in *The Acting Person* (as Wojtyła himself, in fact, so connects it). There the good or value that is the object of an act attains normative force through the recognition of truth by cognition and the intrinsic ordination, or surrender, to truth in the will. Because of this the good necessarily presents itself, in its truth, as a "to be sought or loved." Or, as Wojtyła puts it in a passage from *The Acting Person* quoted in the previous chapter: "In each of his actions the human person is eyewitness of the transition from the 'is' to the 'should'—the transition from 'X is truly good' to 'I should do X'" (*AP*: 162, also 170-71; 'The Person: Subject and Community,' *PC*: 234). Hence not only does it follow that we

48

should treat persons according to what they are—since that is what the good requires that a person by nature is—but it also follows, as Wojtyła says, that others can demand that a person pursue the good in his acts. For that too—requiring that a person behave like a person—must be part of what it means to treat a person as a person. Punishment for wrong doing would presumably fall under this part of the norm, though Wojtyła does not go into any of the details about the nature of punishment (as John Paul II, however, he has said that capital punishment in present conditions is incompatible with the personalistic norm, with human dignity; *Evangelium Vitae* sect. 56).

The norm of treating persons as they are becomes the norm for all dealings with persons, and especially so in the context of the dealings between man and woman. Wojtyła states the norm, in conscious debt to Kant, as a revision of Kant's Categorical Imperative. Kant's Imperative runs:

> Act in such a way that you always treat humanity, whether in your own person or in the person of any other, never simply as a means, but always at the same time as an end.

Wojtyła's runs:

> Whenever a person is the object of your activity, remember that you may not treat that person as only the means to an end, as an instrument, but must allow for the fact that he or she too has, or at least should have, distinct personal ends (*LR:* 27-28).

Wojtyła is careful here not to call the person an end in himself as Kant does. This is no doubt because Kant understands man as having no moral ends given to him by nature or in experience. A man's ends only become moral insofar as he himself makes them moral by not pursuing them beyond what is allowed by Kant's Categorical Imperative, or by the principle that one not demand for oneself in the pursuit of one's own ends any freedom that one is not willing to allow others in the pursuit of their ends. Otherwise those others would not get to act as their own end.

Wojtyła, as a follower of natural law and, indeed, of Scheler, rejects this view. For him action does, prior to and independent of choice, have ends that are moral ends and focus on objective values that are moral values. But, as already explained in the previous chapter, these ends are not external to the person nor are they imposed heteronomously from without, whether by others or one's own passions (as Kant claimed would always be the case with material ends or ends given by experience and not made to be such by us). Instead they are, through the moment of truth just discussed, internal to the subjectivity and freedom of the person. Precisely this fact about the person is denied, however, when a person is used by another as a means to that other's own ends and enjoyment. For then the person's independence, the fact that, as a person, he can and should recognize and follow the good for himself through his own recognition of truth, is violated.

The only acceptable way to treat persons is with love. Love treats the person as an independent being with his own self-determination and his own self-chosen ends. Wojtyła's personalistic norm, in fact, has two aspects to it, a negative and a positive.

> The norm, in its negative aspect, states that the person is the kind of good which does not admit of use and cannot be treated as an object of use and as such the means to an end. In its positive form the personalistic norm confirms this: the person is a good towards which the only proper and adequate attitude is love (*LR:* 41).

The Sexual Urge

This commandment to love is insistent at all times but it has a particular importance in the case of the sexual urge. This urge or instinct is, like all instincts, something that "happens" in man and is not an action but a base for actions, a base, that is, for the exercise of self-determination and of responsibility. Properly understood the urge is not directed to the sexual attributes of someone of the opposite sex but to a human being of the opposite sex. The urge does not exist in abstraction but in concrete individual men and women. Inevitably, therefore, it proceeds from individual to individual, not from sex attribute to sex attribute. If it is directed in some people to sex attributes as such, this must be held to be an impoverishment and a perversion. If it is directed to the sex attributes of someone of the same sex there is homosexual deviation and if to those of an animal there is an even more obvious deviation. But, these deviations aside, the directedness of the sexual urge towards human beings of the opposite sex and the fact that it belongs to what happens in man make it naturally subordinate to and dependent on the person. For it is the person who acts through self-determination and who can understand and make his own the personalisic norm. As *The Acting Person* stressed, the integration of the instinctive elements in man, the psychic and somatic elements, is precisely their being subordinated to (but not suppressed by) the transcendence of the person in self-determination and freedom.

The sexual urge is thus material for action; it does not itself produce complete actions. Acting belongs to the person and is what the person *does*, not what the person *undergoes* through instincts and other happenings in him. The sexual urge is, therefore, human by being integrated into the person, by being made personal. Hence it is only human when it is directed by love for the person and not when it is left at the level of an urge. Nevertheless, or rather for this very reason, the purpose of the urge is not understood from the fact of integration but from *what* it is that is integrated. The sexual urge as a natural reality is for the sake of reproduction, the prolongation of the species. Integration integrates nature into the person; it does not destroy nature. The purpose of reproduction belongs to the sexual urge because of what it is, because of its nature. It is not determined by the human will and is not changeable at will. The work of the will and of self-determination is to integrate this purpose into the person and into love for the person. The sexual urge is not yet love; it is material for love, for a very special kind of love, through integration. Moreover, the urge, even as an urge has an existential and a cosmic significance since through it man and woman enter into "the cosmic stream whereby existence is transmitted" (*LR:* 54). The cosmic significance of the sexual urge is a religious significance but it is religious in the sense that the urge must be seen as a continuation of, and a sharing in, the work of creation. It involves a necessary reference to and a dependence on the Creator. For what a man and woman bring about through reproduction is not just another biological organism; it is a human being who is a unity, a single suppositum, of body and spirit (as Wojtyła argued in *The Acting Person*). The spiritual reality transcends the biological order and its coming to be must ultimately be attributed to the activity of the Creator. Human parents are thus, in their reproductive activity, caught up in co-creation with God of a new human being.

To look, therefore, at sex from the purely biological or scientific point of view is inadequate. But it is no less inadequate to look at it from the point of view of the satisfaction of the libido in Freudian fashion. The sexual urge is not the expression of some pleasure principle; it is not merely or fundamentally an urge to enjoy (though of course enjoyment is necessarily part of its proper use). To think this is to adopt a narrow and purely subjective view of man. It is to absolutize the subjective desire for pleasure and to ignore, or at least to regard as accidental, the orderedness of sex to the transmission of new life. But man is not an instrument of pleasure in this way. He has the capacity to know and comprehend the full objective truth about himself as a real object, a real suppositum, in the world. He can therefore recognize the objective end of the sexual urge, its part in the order of existence and his own place in that order as well as his role in this regard in relation to the Creator.

It would also be an error, an error about the person, to focus wholly on the order of existence and on reproduction and to see the union of male and female as being for that purpose alone. This "rigorist" interpretation would in fact make the spouses into instruments of reproduction and so reduce them to the level of being used. It would be another form of disintegration. Instead of sex being used by persons for their end, the persons would end up being used by sex for its end. But the personalistic dimension must not be allowed to get lost like this. In a true union of persons the natural purpose of the urge becomes the personal purpose of the spouses. It is integrated into their self-determination and becomes part of their freely chosen existence together, of their love for each other. The subjectivity of the spouses' interiority as persons must be united with the objectivity of sexuality (*LR*: 54-66).

It is the latter, however, that is the foundation of conjugal morality. The way Wojtyła expresses this is by drawing a distinction between the aims of marriage and the norm of marriage. The *aims* of marriage are the three traditionally identified: the continuing of existence through children (*procreatio*), conjugal life (*mutuum adiutorium*), and legitimate orientation of desire (*remedium concupiscentiae*). The *norm* of marriage, by contrast, is love. Love is thus not properly an aim of marriage; it is the principle and virtue of marriage. All the aims of marriage must be carried out in love if the marriage is to be personal, a genuine union of persons. But love must, in its turn, respect the objective aims of marriage in order to be a marriage, a sexual union of persons of the opposite sex. Or, as Wojtyła puts it:

> Sexual morality and therefore conjugal morality consists of a stable and mature synthesis of nature's purpose with the personalistic norm (*LR*: 67).

But this is a topic that Wojtyła returns to and elaborates later.

The Nature of Love: Metaphysical Analysis

At this point it would be reasonable to ask what precisely Wojtyła means by love, since love is at the heart of the personalistic norm and is the form and foundation of proper spousal relations between man and woman.

Wojtyła divides his analysis into a metaphysical part, a psychological part, and an ethical part. By the metaphysical part he means the general analysis where elements found in any love are studied. Love between man and woman is a particular kind of love where these general elements are embodied in a special way. The psychological analysis concerns the psyche or, perhaps better, what *The Acting Person* calls the pyschosomatic dimension, where the particular form and differences of the sexual vitality in man and woman, bodily and emotional, are studied. The ethical part concerns the fact that love between persons has a moral character and is ultimately to be seen as a virtue, the greatest of virtues, which raises all others to its own level and imprints on them its own distinctive features.

The metaphysical or general elements of love are identified by Wojtyła as attraction, desire, goodwill, reciprocity, and friendship. To attract someone means, says Wojtyła, more or less to be regarded as a good by the one attracted. This attraction is something cognitive as well as emotive and has an individual character according to the peculiarities of the individuals involved. Truth is thus an important part of attraction, the truth about the value of the persons attracted to each other. This is highlighted by the fact that emotion can distort this truth, and false values are attributed to the person towards whom one is attracted, values that the emotion wants to be there though they are not there in fact. The result when the falseness becomes apparent is disappointment and even hate. Love as attraction is not, therefore, just a matter of the genuineness of the feelings one has towards a person. Certainly the feelings should be there and should be genuine. But the objective truth about the person should be there as well. The two when properly integrated together give to attraction a certain perfection that is part of a genuinely good and genuinely cultivated love.

Love as desire is a need for the other as being a good *for me*. The sexual difference shows up our limits as individual human beings, and the desire of a man for a woman and of a woman for a man are, as it were, an expression of our need for completeness. Desire is therefore self-interested but it is not simply sensual. Its focus is rather on the other person as such, who is conceived as a good for the one desiring. Because the good that satisfies the need thereby has a certain usefulness, the desire could be seen as utilitarian. In fact it is not, or need not be, because it has its rootedness in the personalistic principle and has its focus on the value of the person desired. Love as desire in this sense is, in fact, even present in love for God, since we desire God also as a good for us, but such love of God is not a matter of using God for our own ends.

There is here nevertheless a danger that love as desire could degenerate into something utilitarian if it is not perfected through love as goodwill. Certainly by itself desire is not enough. One must go beyond longing for the other person as a good for oneself and must also, and above all, long for that other person's own good. Goodwill is this longing and it is the purest form of love. It contains no ulterior selfish motive and is inherently altruistic. Love between man and woman cannot help being love of desire, of course, but it must also move, and progressively so, in the direction of goodwill.

Reciprocity is when such love is responded to by the same love in the other so that it exists on both sides and is mutually shared. Love then exists *between*, and not just in, the persons. It is on this basis—that the love of the one for the other is reciprocated by a return of love from the other—that two "I"'s can become a single "We." An unrequited or unreciprocated love would stagnate and be condemned to eventual extinction. Love has to be an interpersonal and not an individual matter. Here one can see how love as desire can go along with love of goodwill. For a person who desires another desires that other as a co-creator of love and not merely as an object of appetite. When such love is genuinely reciprocated and the other does become a co-creator of love, there is a synthesis of love as desire and love as goodwill. If one or both parties, however, felt jealousy or feared unfaithfulness, this would be a sign that love as desire was predominating. Reciprocated love can be of different kinds, depending on what each party contributes to it. If what they contribute is something relatively self-centered the love will be superficial and impermanent. If what they contribute is their personal love, a love focused on the person of the other, and is thus a virtuous love (virtue, as *The Acting Person* argued, is measured by the value of the person, by the personalistic norm), it will be durable and reliable. The parties can then trust each other and are freed from jealousy and suspicion. The fruit of this love is a deep peace and joy. But the trust and the accompanying peace and joy cannot exist when one or both parties have as their end utility or pleasure. It can only exist when the love is of the person for the person's own sake, when it is based on the virtue, however imperfect, of genuine goodwill. Then life together becomes an opportunity for love to grow and to be strengthened by increasing virtue. It becomes a "school of perfection."

Friendship consists in a full commitment of the will to another person with a view to that person's good (that is, in goodwill). It is not the same as sympathy though it is accompanied and even preceded by sympathy. Sympathy is properly a feeling, an "experiencing together" with another. As such it betokens both an element of community (there is a togetherness about it) and an element of passivity (it is a feeling not an acting). It is something that happens in man and not something that man does through choice and will. People can therefore succumb to it and be drawn to one another by the pull of emotions and not by conscious choice. This is love at an emotional stage without any commitment of the will and without any necessary reference to the objective value of the person. It has its place in love because it brings people together and makes them feel together; it is the empirical and palpable manifestation of love. But it is not the whole of love. Love must become friendship, the mutual commitment of wills, if it is to endure. Friendship is a personal act of choice, not a mere happening, and it engages the whole human being. But it needs sympathy to supply it with the emotional warmth that is proper to the human subject. The two things should go together: sympathy needs to be transformed into friendship and friendship needs to be supplemented by sympathy. That is why love must not be left at the stage of sympathy, where it typically begins and often with great intensity too. The sympathy must be actively and consciously molded into friendship; it cannot be left at the level of the feeling. It is a mistake to measure love by sympathy and to think that the two come and go together. Sympathy is only the beginning. There is a positive need here for a proper education in love, a true art of loving, which would teach the need to transform sympathy into friendship. A lack of such education, thinks Wojtyła, is the reason for many disasters in human love. Moreover, without this transformation into friendship or the union of wills of two people, the proper basis for marriage and family is not there. The couple have not fused their separate "I"s into a single "We." A couple need to have a common objective interest and not just be united by common subjective feelings. Love may be a subjective thing and reside in personal subjects, but it must be free of subjectivism. It must relate to objective goods and reflect real acts of choice. Only thus can it be personal (in the sense of *The Acting Person*) and measure up to the demands of the personalistic norm (*LR:* 73-100).

Wojtyła introduces here the complementary idea of betrothed love. He describes this as the giving of one's person to another, as the self-giving, the surrender, of one's I (*LR:* 96). Such self-giving can in fact be found outside spousal love, as in the devotion of a mother to her child, or in the relationship of a doctor to his patient, of a teacher to his pupils, or of a pastor to the souls in his care. It exists, however, in a special and luminous way in matrimony which is precisely the self-giving of a man and woman to each other in a total way (a parallel would be to the total giving of oneself to God). The mere giving of oneself sexually without the full gift of one's person would amount to a using of the other (and of oneself) and would be a denial of the personalistic norm. Only reciprocal self-giving can bring marriage within the requirements of that norm.

The self-gift of one person to another (whether in marriage or elsewhere) actually contains in it a certain paradox for Wojtyła. For self-gift means making oneself over to be, in a way, another's property, and yet it is a cardinal thesis of Wojtyła's personalism that the person cannot belong to another but is always his own possession. The personalistic norm is built on this claim. An answer, which Wojtyła hints at rather than develops, can be drawn from the analyses of *The Acting Person*. First of all the gift of self is something in the moral order and not the natural or physical order (voluntary slavery would perhaps be self-gift in the physical order and doubtless Wojtyła would understand that to be directly excluded by the personalistic norm). Secondly the way the self is understood in Wojtyła's phenomenology of the person is that it is constituted in the suppositum through acting and the full exercise of self-determination. In particular, participation is the acting together of two or more persons who, through such joint action, are constituting, as it were, a joint self. Each is thus energizing his personal freedom (which only the person himself controls) in the service of the other's energizing of his personal freedom. This amounts to self-gift in the sense that the self that is constituted through that action (or through that whole life of action in the case of marital self-gift) is given to the other so that both may, as regards their realization in that action at least, be one self and be jointly realized and fulfilled in that one self. The one is being constituted in the other as the other is being constituted in that one. At least this is the way that Wojtyła's phenomenology suggests that he understands the notion of self-gift. His remarks on participation point in that direction, and the following passage from *Love and Responsibility* seems to contain the substance of the idea:

> Before their love can take on its definitive form, become 'betrothed love', the man and the woman each face the choice of the person on whom to bestow the gift...The object of choice is another person, but it is as though one were choosing another 'I', choosing oneself in another, and the other in oneself...[A] human being is always first and foremost himself ('a person'), and in order not merely to live with another but to live by and for that other person he must continually discover himself in the other and the other in himself...[O]nly the spirituality and inwardness of persons create the conditions for mutual interpenetration, which enables each to live in and by the other (*LR:* 131; 'Participation and Alienation,' *PC:* 200-202).

The Nature of Love: Psychological and Ethical Analysis

As regards the psychological elements of love, or its emotional side (to the extent that this has not already been covered in the metaphysical analysis), Wojtyła first describes emotion in love as an experience of the other as a value, a positive good (reference to good and bad seems necessarily included in the idea of emotional response, as *The Acting Person* argues). The two emotions or emotional factors he identifies in the case of love between man and woman are sensuality and sentiment, of which the former seems to be stronger in man and the latter in woman. Both can lead to problems if they are not fully integrated into the self-determination of the person. Sensuality leads to a consumerist response to the person of the opposite sex and focuses on the body and the sexual use of the body rather than on the person. Sentiment is, by contrast, focused on the whole person but its danger is that it paints the beloved in false colors and depicts him according to some impossible or at least unreal image. Disillusionment is then the more or less inevitable result, and all the more so when, as is not seldom the case for the woman, she discovers that sentiment in man is a screen for sensuality and for the will to use her.

Both emotional factors are, however, necessary and have an indispensable place in love and sexuality. But they are material for love rather than love itself. Here Wojtyła's teaching on integration becomes especially important. These factors, like emotions generally, must, if they are to play their proper role in male-female relations, be integrated into the person and become subordinate to his free self-determination with its focus on truth and therewith on the personalistic norm. The truth about the value of the person, one's own and others, must guide and fuse sensuality and sentiment into genuine love. Genuine love is always the affirmation of the value of the person; it is a "love in which sexual values are subordinated to the value of the person" (*LR:* 101-18).

The nature and need of such integration brings Wojtyła directly to the ethical elements of love, which have, in their essence, already been set out. The duty, inherent in the structure of the will and freedom, to choose the true good means that love must be focused on the person (not the body), and that love as an experience must be subordinate to love as a virtue, that is, to a deliberate and developed choice of the person and the good of the person for the person's own sake. In any choice there is a commitment of freedom and therefore in some sense a limitation too (to choose this person as spouse is necessarily to "forsake all other"). But freedom actually exists for the sake of such commitment, for the sake, that is, of love. Freedom is, as it were, the means and love the end. But this love, this gift of self to the other, is actually the fulfillment of freedom and of the person since that is what they are for. Freedom *wants* to commit itself. Hence love as self gift of person to person must precede and be the basis for the sexual and emotional elements of love. They must be founded on it and not vice versa. Otherwise one will lose the personalism of love and fall back into some naturalism or biologism or libidinism. The person in his free self-determination is the fundamental truth of man (as *The Acting Person* showed at length). The rest must be integrated into that and not it collapsed into them. Hence true love is not led by the sexual instinct but leads it and assumes responsibility for it and for its inherent purpose.

But there is a religious aspect to all this too. To love is ultimately to desire unlimited good, good without qualification, for the other, and that in the end can be nothing else than God himself. This is part of love as a virtue in contrast to love as an emotion or an instinct. As a virtue, however, love is an ongoing task that necessarily involves education. It is a great work of persons—a way in which a man learns to live up to his high dignity as a free person called to full gift of self in love. Such love between man and woman has as one of its special tasks guarding against its own disintegration, that is to say, preventing the material and emotional aspects of love from falling out of their place in, and their subordination to, the free self gift of the person (*LR:* 118-40).

Chastity and Shame

Here Wojtyła appeals to the virtue of chastity. This virtue has been much maligned and even "outlawed" from the soul, will, and heart of man. The reason for this is not, however, any discovery of some previously unknown truth in man or sexuality; rather it is due to resentment (at this point Wojtyła picks up on some work of Max Scheler). Resentment is a feature of the *subjective mentality* where pleasure (emotional, physical) takes the place of superior values. It arises from a distorted sense of values and has its origin in weakness of will. It is a sort of hatred of the good because the good is hard and requires a great effort of will. And, of course, true love in the form of self-gift is both a great good and hard. It is not surprising, therefore, that such love and its distinctive virtues should excite resentment. Chastity is the particular object of resentment in this regard since it operates more than anything against the pursuit of mere pleasure in love.

Chastity is, however, very necessary in genuine love. It betokens purity, and its function is to make love clear and to liberate from everything that makes love dirty. What Wojtyła means here is that we must always be able to "see through" all the sensations and actions of lovers to the fact that their love is based on a sincere affirmation of the person, or that it is true personal love. Chastity does this above all because it fights to prevent concupiscence or sensuality from dominating, which would inevitably lead to use of the beloved and not to affirmation of the person. It would muddy love which instead of being transparent in its focusing on the person would become a cloak to hide a mere utilitarian desire. Concupiscence unchecked would subvert all the values of true love. Chastity works to integrate concupiscence and sensual desire into love of the person. It works, in other words, to keep them pure and formed as they should be—subordinate to the truth about the person and about sex. It not only protects one's own person, therefore, against the destructive influence of irrational forces within oneself, but also, since love joins two persons, it protects one's beloved too from that same destructive influence. In sum chastity "consists in quickness to affirm the value of the person in every situation, and in raising to the personal level all reactions to the body and sex" (*LR:* 171, 143-73).

The components of chastity as so understood are identified by Wojtyła as shame and continence (or moderation). Shame arises "when something which of its very nature or in view of its purpose ought to be private passes the bounds of a person's privacy and somehow becomes public." Or again: "Shame is a tendency, uniquely characteristic of the human person, to conceal sexual values sufficiently to prevent them from obscuring the value of the person as such" (*LR:* 174, 187). Shame thus has an immediate application to the love of man and woman because, as already emphasized, sexual activity is only human when it is integrated into the person and the subjectivity of the person's inwardness in self-gift. The love between man and woman is thus primarily an internal reality that only they themselves are fully privy to. Others can of course see the external manifestation of this love but they do not, by definition, enter into the inwardness that belongs to the couple themselves. The sexual act and the sexual parts of the body, if displayed to others, would thus only be manifest in their externality; the inwardness of their integration into love of the person would not be thus manifest. Hence such public display would be matter for shame because it would fail "to conceal sexual values sufficiently to prevent them from obscuring the value of the person as such." The persons instead would be displayed for others as using each other and as objects of use for each other.

Such sexual shame is thus not found in children at an age at which sexual values do not exist for them. But shame, and modesty, should and do naturally arise in children as they mature. Shame follows, however, a different course in the two sexes because of the difference, mentioned before, of the psychological structures in man and woman. Since sensuality, or the orientation to the body as "an object of enjoyment," is generally stronger and more importunate in men, there is a special need not only of restraint in men but also of modesty and shame in women, so that men are not seduced into treating female bodies as such objects. On the other hand, since women tend to be less aware of sensuality in themselves and of its natural orientation in men, they tend not to feel this need for modesty or of the need, in the presence of men, to conceal the body as a potential object of enjoyment. "The evolution of modesty in women," Wojtyła therefore concludes, "requires some insight into the male psychology" (*LR:* 177).

Of course in true committed love between spouses there is no longer place for shame in their sexual relations with each other. Here shame is absorbed by love. For once love, true personal love, is in place, sexual values have necessarily been integrated and the body of the other does not descend to the level of being a mere object for use and enjoyment. Shame thus clears the way for love. For while love between man and woman begins and develops on the basis of sexual values, it must in the end be based on the right attitude towards the value of the person. Shame, by keeping sexual values under a suitable veil, helps to ensure that this process to the personal level does actually occur and is not hijacked along the way, as it were, and kept back at the sexual level alone. It thus prepares the way for its own absorption into love when the sexual values have been integrated into and subordinated to the self gift of person to person. Despite its great value, however, in fostering true love between men and women, sexual shame is easily derailed, both from within and from without. There is need, therefore, for the young in particular to be educated in sexual shame. Shame should in fact form an integral part of their sex education.

As for the other part of chastity, moderation or continence, this is the "ability to find that mean in the control of sexual excitability and sentimental impressionability which will best facilitate the realization of love and avoid the dangers of exploitation" (*LR*: 195-96). The person has a special need to defend himself against emotional stirrings that threaten the natural power of self-determination. Everything is for the sake of the person and of the transcendence of the person through authentic integration. Moderation is thus fundamentally in accordance with nature (*LR*: 168), as indeed is shame and their joint realization in chastity. They preserve the person in the recognition and pursuit of objective values and of the truth of love and the person (*LR*: 194-208).

One can readily draw quite definite conclusions from these analyses. Wojtyła himself draws such conclusions about dress, pornography, and art. There is going to be a certain relativity here, of course, according to differences of person, place, and custom, but there are also, beneath these differences, certain abiding principles. So immodesty in dress, for instance, is "that which frankly contributes to the deliberate displacement of the person by sexual values, that which is bound to elicit a reaction to the person as to a possible means of obtaining sexual enjoyment and not a possible object of love by reason of his or her personal value" (*LR*: 190) This is a clear statement and a clear principle that would require many changes in contemporary practice. Nevertheless it is important to note that it does not specify any particular dress code. That is left for particular decision in particular

61

cases. Wojtyła allows, for instance, that there are situations where partial or even total nudity is not immodest (as in the case of physical labor, bathing, or a medical examination). Forms of dress must be judged starting from the function they serve—providing always, of course, that the principle just stated is followed.

As for pornography or shamelessness in art, Wojtyła notes that art does not only communicate the artist's feelings and attitudes, it also serves the truth in that it "must capture and transmit some fragment of reality in a beautiful way" (*LR:* 192). Wojtyła, one should recall, is himself a poet and so presumably speaks out of direct personal experience here. One such fragment of reality that artists often try to capture is the love of man and woman, and of course the body is part of this reality. What would be wrong in artistic renderings of such love would be to focus on the bodily part at the expense of the whole phenomenon, or focus on it in such a way as to obscure the whole and make the part seem a whole by itself and not the fragment that it really is. This is what pornography in art does, for instance. It accentuates the sexual element and induces the audience or viewer to believe that sexual values are the only values of the person, and that love is nothing but the experience of these values alone. The harm here is evident from all that has been summarized above. Pornography distorts the truth about sex and about human love by disintegrating sex from the whole of the person and giving it a false independence. By the same token, of course, pornography distorts the truth about art. It separates art from the truth about the part of reality that art seeks to transmit.

What is striking about this analysis of Wojtyła's is that his criticism of art is primarily an artistic and not a moral one. Pornography is bad art *before* it is morally corrupting art, and it is bad art because it is not focused on the truth of its object. That this lack of truth is also a moral harm is because, in addition, it offends the personalistic norm. But art could presumably be false without also offending this norm (say if it focused on some object that had no direct reference to persons). It would then be bad art without being immoral art. By contrast, immoral art could never fail to be bad art. For art could not be immoral without offending the personalistic norm and it could not offend this norm without denying some truth about the person that it was taking for its object. For the norm is precisely an expression of the truth about the person. Technical deficiency in art, however, would seem to be a third thing (though Wojtyła says nothing about this). A failure in draftsmanship or in harmonization, for instance, would produce technically bad painting and music, but it need not, as such, distort the truth of its object or offend the personalistic norm.

Marriage

Such ethical consequences of Wojtyła's personalism are clear enough. There are others that are equally clear, especially in the context of marriage. They concern: the exclusivity of marriage; the indissolubility of marriage; the social and religious context of marriage; the indissoluble tie between sexual activity on the one hand and reproduction and the union of persons on the other. All these are related to and founded on the truth about human sexual love and about the person. They are also striking instances of Wojtyła's creative fusion of personalism and natural law, or rather of his *personalizing* of natural law.

The love of man and woman, if it is to be a union of persons who, according to the personalistic norm, may never be a mere object of use or enjoyment, needs a suitable framework. This framework is marriage understood as monogamous and indissoluble. If a man and woman unite as persons and the focus of love is the other person, it must continue as long as the person continues. For if it ended while the person continued it would not have been focused on the person after all but on something else—something else that could come and go while the person lasted. Since the person ends, at least as far as the specific union of marriage is concerned, only with the death of the body (for marriage connotes a union of bodies), death and death alone is the proper terminus of marriage. Remarriage is then possible and compatible with the personalistic norm, but consecrated widowhood (or widowerhood) is specially praiseworthy because it emphasizes the reality of the union with the deceased person. This is because of the spiritual independence of the person from matter and therefore also, in principle, from bodily death (*LR:* 212). A married couple could nevertheless, for sufficiently serious reasons, separate while each was alive, but that would not dissolve the marriage. Marriage has an objective reality once contracted that no subsequent changes of circumstances or will can dissolve. Otherwise, as noted above, the personalistic norm would be violated (*LR:* 214).

Monogamy is also a requirement of marriage. Since the union of one man with one woman is already sufficient for a full union of persons, there could be no need, as far as this goes, for another union of the same sort with another person at the same time. Any further need would either be for numerous progeny (as with the Old Testament

Patriarchs), or for sexual use, and both of these ends, if made the object of the union, necessarily offend the personalistic norm. So if the personalistic norm is to be observed in its fullness, as becomes the dignity of the person, marriage has to be monogamous.

Marriage must also be a social institution and not a mere private commitment between the spouses. For, as Wojtyła argued in the discussion of participation in *The Acting Person*, man is a social being and his existence and action inevitably have a social character. Hence there is a need, a felt need, to make marriage public and to sanction it in a public way. The relationship of the spouses is justified and legitimated for them, of course, through their genuine love for each other as persons (for only thus does their love fulfill the personalistic norm and satisfy the objective order of justice set up by that norm). But because of man's social character, the spouses also need to have this justification and legitimation recognized, respected, and fostered by their family, friends, and the wider community. This is what public marriage does. Such open witness of love is all the more necessary in view of the offspring that are the natural fruit of marriage. For children are themselves new members of society and, through them, the marriage becomes a family, which is itself a society and the basis of all larger societies (nation, state, church). Hence for all these reasons marriage must find its reflection in the practices and law of those larger societies. And this is what it means for marriage to be an institution.

> In a society which accepts sound ethical principles and lives in accordance with them..., this institution is necessary to signify the maturity of the union between a man and a woman, to testify that theirs is a love on which a lasting union and community can be based (*LR:* 220).

There is also a special reference to religion involved here. Religion is not properly a matter of having or being capable of certain experiences (as people tend to suppose). Rather it is a matter of justice toward the Creator. To be created, says Wojtyła, means to depend on another, the Creator, for one's existence. Wojtyła does not, of course, discuss any proofs for God and creation in this context since that would take him too far afield. He has to take them for granted. But assuming they are in place we must conclude that a complete personalism and a complete account of personal love between man and woman could not omit the fact that persons and their acts depend on God for their existence. Marriage, therefore, must not only receive a social sanction but a religious one too, so that the due of justice is paid to God (*LR:* 223).

Marriage, of course, is a union of persons in their sexuality as well as in their persons, and this too carries ethical consequences with it. The chief and most profound one that conditions all the others is that of integration. The sexual union is integrated into the personal union and cannot be separated from it without offending the personalistic norm. But the stress here must be on the term *integration*. To integrate means that the sexual act, with all its natural and biological reality, is taken up into the love of persons. Integration does not mean that sexuality gets changed from what it naturally is into something else. Integration is not change but subsumption. Consequently sex is not something that a couple may use as they wish. On the contrary they may only use it according to what it naturally is. Here the natural order and the personal order meet. When a couple united in marriage choose to engage in sexual activity, they are choosing to engage in the creation of new life. This is not just a matter of the nature of sex; it is a matter of love of the person too. For the human person is a sexual being and to love the person is to love everything about the person, including the objective truth of their sexuality or the fact that written into sexual activity is the possibility of parenthood (*LR:* 226-30).

These facts clearly rule out from sexual relations any interference with the sexual activity that would render it incapable of producing offspring (for that would, effectively, be to de-sex sex). One is talking here of interference in the sexual act, not of the natural rhythm of sexuality. Since it is part of the order of nature and of sexuality that this order "leaves the connection between the sexual act and reproduction in particular marriages a matter of some uncertainty" (*LR:* 233), it would be absurdly strict, even unnatural, to demand that every sexual act be actually procreative, or to say that intercourse is only permissible if the couple hope to have a child as a result of it. To use nature's order is very different from breaking nature's order. Natural family planning, therefore, or periodic abstinence and the use of the woman's natural infertility to space the birth of children, would be perfectly legitimate. Such periodic abstinence is not a mere technique; it is or should be a virtue, the virtue of love and continence. It is an expression, indeed, of the personalism of marriage, or of the fact that the self gift of the spouses to each other is a personal union that gives to sexual intercourse a necessary role in the fostering of love and not just in procreation. It is also an expression of the fact that marriage is grounded on the affirmation of the value of the person and that married love, to be mature, must ripen to the point where the exercise of the virtue of continence is possible and where it is one of the factors giving shape to the whole pattern of the couple's love. Inability or refusal to abstain, even for good reason, must betoken some sort of distortion of love away from the person toward mere sexuality. (*LR:* 231-44, 282).

By the same token, of course, it now follows that if, because of the integration of the nature of sex into personal union, nothing may be done to exclude the procreative aspect from sex, then it also follows that nothing may be done to exclude the nature of sex from the personal union into which it must be integrated. The reproduction of children outside the context of the union of the spouses necessarily, therefore, offends the personalistic norm as much as artificial contraception offends it. Wojtyła does not discuss this aspect explicitly in *Love and Responsibility*, but it is clear that his philosophy of the person would exclude, for instance, *in vitro* fertilization, surrogate motherhood, cloning and so forth. This is not because such things offend biology (on the contrary they make special use of biology), but because they absolutize biology and denigrate both the person and nature (*LR* p. 226; 'The Problem of Catholic Sexual Ethics,' *PC:* 294).

One can see here above all the creative character of Wojtyła's use of the traditional teaching of natural law. He does not proceed simply from the nature of the sexual act but rather from this nature as integrated into the person. Wojtyła finds this already in *Humanae Vitae*, that enormously controversial encyclical of Pope Paul VI condemning artificial birth control. For *Humanae Vitae* speaks not only of the meaning of the conjugal act that results from an understanding of its nature, but also of the *intended* meaning, or the meaning that the spouses themselves give to the act. They should signify in their act the meaning that the act itself has and not some other meaning. This is, of course, a way of speaking about integration, of the fact that the objective realities of the body must be taken up into the self-determination of the person. Wojtyła therefore sees a genuine personalism in Paul VI's encyclical and even speaks of it as passing from "a theology of nature to a theology of person." ('The Teaching of *Humanae Vitae* on Love,' *PC:* 301-14, 308; 'The Problem of Catholic Sexual Ethics,' *PC:* 293-97). It is striking, and a tribute to the intensity of Wojtyła's personalism, that whereas most other commentators have found in the encyclical only a repetition of the traditional teaching of natural law, he has found there a fusing of that teaching with a genuine insight into the person, or rather a creative raising of it to the plane of the person. At all events, it would be false to accuse Wojtyła, or

Wojtyła's Paul VI, of biologism in the matter of sexual ethics. Wojtyła's approach is thoroughly personalistic and holistic: one that takes account of and accepts both the order of the person and the order of nature. Those who would, in the name of the person, sanction the rejection or breaking of the order of nature, are themselves failing to see the fact of integration. They are effectively adopting, argued Wojtyła later as John Paul II, a dualistic view of man and are divorcing body and nature from the person, whereas the two are in reality a single whole (*Veritatis Splendor:* sects. 47-50).

As confirmation of all this, we may note that Wojtyła ends his book with some reflections on the scientific facts about the body and sex. Part of the aim of these reflections is to show that, far from opposing such facts and causing physical or psychological problems as some allege, his personalistic and integral approach is fully in accordance with these facts. Physical and psychological health are preserved in personalism and not otherwise. It is those who would separate sex from the person, says Wojtyła, who are producing neuroses and ill health. Interesting in this regard is that Wojtyła's only remarks on abortion in *Love and Responsibility* are not about what it does to the child but about what it does to the woman:

> The act of artificially terminating a pregnancy is in itself highly 'traumatic', and in every respect comparable with those experiments which are designed to produce neuroses. It is indeed an artificial interruption of the natural biological rhythm with very far-reaching consequences. There is no analogy for the enormous feeling of resentment which it leaves in the mind of the woman...Apart from its physical effects artificial abortion causes an anxiety neurosis with guilt feelings at its core, and sometimes even a profound psychotic reaction (*LR:* 284-85).

Wojtyła was writing this in 1960, a decade or more before abortion became widely practiced in the West. But Poland, like other communist bloc countries, had long had legalized abortion. Wojtyła is evidently writing out of that experience and so had seen by 1960 and before what the Western nations have only seen, and only admitted with great reluctance, in the last decades. He is doubtless also speaking out of his experience as a spiritual guide and confessor (*LR:* 15). His personalism, one feels, is not only a matter of theory; it is also a matter of his own concrete lived experience.

5

Philosophical Theology

Philosophy and Theology

Theology is not the same as philosophy and a book on Wojtyła's philosophy ought to be cautious about crossing the line into his theology. But there are two reasons not to avoid crossing the line altogether. The first is a general one about philosophy itself and the second a specific one about Wojtyła the man.

Philosophy in its literal and original meaning is simply love of wisdom (*philo-sophia*), a love of wisdom anywhere and everywhere it is to be found. In this sense there are no limits on philosophy and philosophy identifies itself with any study whatever. Every systematic investigation of truth is philosophy: science, art, craft. Consequently theology is philosophy too. Indeed it will be the peak and perfection of philosophy if God, whom theology studies, is the peak and perfection of wisdom. Theology traditionally divides, however, into natural theology and revealed theology. Natural theology is the study and knowledge of God that can be achieved through the use of unaided reason alone. Examples of such theology can be found in classical philosophical writings, such as Aristotle's and Descartes' works on metaphysics. Revealed theology, by contrast, is the study and knowledge of God that is based on divine revelation and can be achieved only through a use of reason aided by revelation. Such theology may be said to be theology in its standard or more recognized sense. In this sense it is distinguished from philosophy. But this

68

distinction between two kinds of theology, and between theology and philosophy, postdates the Ancient World where philosophy began and postdates much of the Medieval World too. The reason is the original meaning of philosophy, that philosophy is the love of wisdom wherever and however it is to be found. For from this perspective the fact that some truth about God can be known by reason without extra divine help and that other truth about him can be known by reason only with such help makes no difference to the love of wisdom. Such love will welcome wisdom from every source including and perhaps especially from divine revelation. One might think of Socrates in Plato's *Apology* (23a5-b4), or of Parmenides at the beginning of his famous poem, or of Aristotle in the *Eudemian Ethics* (1248a16-b7). Revealed theology would thus be philosophy finally perfected, or as perfected as God, through his revelation, had chosen to make it. This way of understanding revealed theology is recognized by Wojtyła himself as John Paul II in his encyclical *Fides et Ratio* (chapter 4), though, of course, he recognizes the other and more usual way too. At all events, there is, on this understanding, no difficulty but rather a certain propriety for a book on Wojtyła's philosophy to pass from philosophy to revealed theology, for this is to pass, in a way, from philosophy to philosophy.

The second reason to consider Wojtyła's theology in a book on his philosophy is the man himself. I do not just mean here the fact that Wojtyła is the same man who wrote both, but much more the fact that Wojtyła's theology is directly continuous with his philosophy and develops from it and through it. Both are extended reflections on the being of the human person as this manifests itself to us in lived experience, whether the lived experience be that of the natural man or also of the man of faith. To do justice, therefore, to the philosophy of Wojtyła requires one to say something about the way it feeds into the theology of Wojtyła. But a word of caution is in order here. Wojtyła the theologian is also primarily the Cardinal Archbishop of Cracow and Pope John Paul II. His writings as Cardinal Archbishop can fairly be regarded as his own, albeit in an official Church capacity. But his writings, or his official writings, as John Paul II must primarily be seen as documents of the Church's highest teaching authority. In his papal encyclicals (usually the most important of a pope's official writings) Wojtyła speaks not as Wojtyła but as Vicar of Christ and Pastor of the Universal Church. Moreover these writings, although they appear under his name and possess authority because they do so, are not simply works of his personal authorship. They are collaborative writings and reflect the mind of others too. Still, they are his as official and authoritative author, and it is as such that they will be discussed here. Further they will be discussed, or some of them will be discussed, only insofar as they manifest, reflect, and develop the phenomenological personalism of Wojtyła and not in their totality. Philosophy in its narrower sense of the work of unaided reason must, in a book devoted primarily to Wojtyła's philosophy in this narrower sense, be the guiding measure if not the whole subject matter. For in fact we find in Wojtyła's theological writings a noteworthy instance of philosophy aiding faith to express itself, or of philosophy as handmaid or, perhaps better, as midwife to theology. Seeing how Wojtyła makes his philosophy do this is already itself a matter of no little philosophical interest. It is a matter of no less philosophical interest to see how, in line with his own remarks as John Paul II in *Fides et Ratio* (sect. 77), his use of philosophy as handmaid or *ancilla theologiae* is in no way meant to be a distortion of philosophy but rather to be a special kind of application of it. In this respect such use of philosophy is not altogether unlike its use in what we now call applied or practical ethics, as in business ethics or medical ethics. True, Wojtyła applies it to revelation, to something that, unlike business or medicine, is not accessible to unaided reason. But it is still application that Wojtyła is aiming to do and not abuse or manipulation.

Personalizing the Church: The Second Vatican Council

John Paul II is a pope formed by and loyal to the teaching of the Second Vatican Council (1962-65). It is the documents of that council that have directed his reflections, his actions, and his official teachings. To them he constantly returns and from them he constantly takes inspiration and guidance. But that was true of him already before he became pope. In fact his philosophical personalism received confirmation and stimulus from those documents as well as a certain expression in them. *The Acting Person* was in part written while Wojtyła was attending Vatican II as one of the bishops and fathers of it (*AP:* 302 n9). But the main proof of the connection between the Council and Wojtyła's personalism is to be found in what he himself later wrote about the Council and its implementation as Archbishop of Cracow in a work entitled *Sources of Renewal: the Implementation of Vatican II*. Most of this work consists of quotations from the documents of the Council with comments by Wojtyła which are designed, in the first instance, to assist the Church of Cracow to realize and follow out what Vatican II said and recommended. As such it needs no special discussion here. But what does need discussion here, and what is so striking about the book, is the fundamentally personalist way in which Wojtyła reads the Council and understands the message it wants implemented. Indeed, the book is really a sort of phenomenology of the Church understood as a community or a communion of persons constituting the People of God. It is about the Church's consciousness of itself as that People or even about the Church's *Self* as such. That the Council saw itself as primarily pastoral and not dogmatic, as primarily guiding the People of God into an enrichment of their lived faith rather than as expounding dogmas for intellectual assent, confirms Wojtyła in his interpretation of it. That interpretation may not unfairly be dubbed "The Acting People of God."

Vatican II, then, is about enriching the faith, and implementing Vatican II in this regard Wojtyła understands to be a matter of *consciousness* and *attitudes*. He divides his book into three parts: an introductory part on the meaning of enrichment of faith, or on what he also calls "Conciliar Initiation," a second part on the formation of consciousness, and a final part on the formation of attitudes.

As regards the introductory part, the enrichment of faith of which Wojtyła speaks is not, he repeats, primarily a matter of correct definitions of dogma or clarifications of the sense of certain doctrines. It is not about the intellectual object of faith; it is not objective, in this sense. Rather it is subjective in the sense of being about what it is like in concrete terms to be a believer: what the existential reality is, or the lived experience if you will, of being a believer. This is a difficult and complex question because:

> it not only presupposes the truth of faith and pure doctrine but also calls for that truth to be situated in the human consciousness and calls for a definition of the attitude, or rather the many attitudes, that go to make the individual a believing member of the Church (*SR:* 17-18).

What is at issue is giving Christians "a life-style, a way of thinking and acting." One can hardly mistake here already the fundamentally personalist reading that Wojtyła gives to the Council.

Faith, to begin with, is understood both as God's gift and also as man's conscious attitude. It is God's gift because his revelation, his self-revelation, of himself to man is a gratuitous act on God's part.

Man's response to this revelation is also God's gift for, while this response is in man, it does not originate from man; it originates from God. The response takes the form, not merely of an assent to certain truths, but of the abandonment of one's whole self to God. It touches man's "whole personal structure and spiritual dynamism." Thus it is, to be sure, an effect of divine grace, but it is also a fully human and personal act; it is "essentially supernatural" and at the same time "strictly personal" (SR 23). It is, in fact, an exercise, a perfect exercise, of man's free self-determination, that fundamental and defining aspect of man explored in *The Acting Person.* Wojtyła's focus is both on what this conscious attitude of faith is a consciousness of, namely on what truths, and also, and much more, on what sort of experienced act it is in the person who performs it. In this regards Wojtyła sees the act of faith as having both a vertical and a horizontal dimension (*SR:* 37, 91,112).

By vertical and horizontal dimension here Wojtyła does not mean what he meant in *The Acting Person* when he spoke of vertical and horizontal transcendence as structural characteristics of the free act of a person, a self-determining agent. He is talking rather of kinds of participation. Nevertheless the vertical and horizontal structure of transcendence has, of course, to be presupposed to the act of faith which is, as any human act must be, a free determination of self (vertical transcendence) towards objective truth (horizontal transcendence). Wojtyła is keeping this structure in mind in *Sources of Renewal,* for, as he says, faith, understood as self-abandonment to God, implies that "man has the free disposal of himself" (*SR:* 20). Or, as he again says, "man brings his own freedom into religion and commits himself, accepting as truth the word of God and the self-revelation of God which it contains" (*SR:* 23). But what marks the act of faith as an act of faith, over and above its being a matter of self-determination, is that it is an instance of self-gift or self-abandonment to God himself. This idea obviously recalls the similar idea of self-gift analyzed in *Love and Responsibility,* and also brings us into the structure of participation analyzed in *The Acting Person.* Putting the several elements together we may say that the act of faith is a participating by man in the life, or indeed, the *Self* of God (Wojtyła does not use this expression but it is, I think, a fair reflection of his meaning). Such participating would be the vertical dimension of faith, the gift that man makes of himself to God. It is at once followed by and conditions the horizontal dimension of faith which is the gift that man, now constituted as believer, makes of himself to his fellow believers. This gift of himself to them and of them to him is what makes all together into the one People of God and is itself a kind of participation. Both kinds of participation—the vertical to God and the horizontal to the People of God—deserve discussion, but the vertical one first since it is the cause and origin and indispensably continuing context of the second. To lose the vertical dimension by infidelity or sin is at once to lose the horizontal dimension, at least in its spiritual reality, because it is to lose the reality of being a believer who can, in his act of believing, give himself to other believers in their act of believing.

As regards the vertical dimension, then, one should recall, as already noted, that believing or the act of faith is "not merely the response of the mind to an abstract truth;" rather it engages "man's whole personal structure and spiritual dynamism" (*SR:* 20). Or, to quote the words Wojtyła used as John Paul II in *Fides et Ratio* (sect. 13):

> [T]he act of trusting oneself to God [is] a moment of fundamental decision which engages the whole person. In that act, the intellect and the will display their spiritual nature, enabling the subject to act in a way which realizes personal freedom to the full.

One therefore has to view faith, in its lived and subjective reality in the believer, as "a state of consciousness and an attitude," as a "conscious response to the God who reveals himself" (*SR:* 27). This response does have a content to which assent is made, the content of the truth in which God reveals himself. So there have to be dogmas and there has to be an acknowledged teaching authority. But that is not Wojtyła's focus. His focus is on the kind of response it is; his focus is on the subject and not the object of belief. As he says:

> 'The obedience of faith' is not bound to any particular faculty...Man's response to God consists in self-abandonment to God. This is the true dimension of faith, in which man does not simply accept a particular set of propositions, but accepts his own vocation...The believer's whole existence constitutes his response to the gift of God which is revelation...The postulate of conscious faith...is nothing but a constant concern on man's part to respond to the God who reveals himself (*SR:* 20, 24).

This response is, as has been said, a question of consciousness and attitudes and in both respects it is a total self-giving to God. By consciousness Wojtyła means awareness and above all self-awareness. It is not the acknowledgement of certain truths (for that the term 'knowledge' would surely be enough) but the absorption, as it were, of these truths into oneself so that one becomes who one is as a believer through them; so that one becomes aware of oneself in one's believing as fundamentally formed in one's being, one's real existence, by what, or rather by whom, the truths reveal.

Wojtyła divides this consciousness into consciousness of creation (of oneself and the world as made by God), of salvation (of God as revealing himself as a Trinity of persons whose life man is called to share), and of redemption (of Christ as God incarnate come to lead men into that divine life). These elements of consciousness strictly form the mind of the believer and the Church. They are the fashioning elements of how the believer sees himself precisely as a believer, precisely as one who is wholly abandoned to the God who reveals himself. What Wojtyła says about these elements as they are found in the documents of Vatican II needs no special comment here. His remarks more or less repeat what the documents say and what the Church has always taught. They are a sort of doctrinal catechesis. What does deserve comment, however, is how this vertical consciousness of the believer upwards to God as Creator and Savior is seen by Wojtyła to create and condition the horizontal consciousness of the believer outward to the whole body of believers in the one People of God.

The People of God is the communion of persons who, in one way or another, have responded in an act of self-abandonment to the self-revealing God. This communion therefore makes no sense, and has no being, apart from the relation of the individual believer to God. Thus just as the vertical dimension to God is prior in nature to and the sustaining source of the horizontal dimension, so the individual formed as a believer by his response to God is prior in nature to the communion of such persons that is the People of God.

> The consciousness of the Church as the People of God is profoundly permeated by the consciousness of personal vocation...God converts human beings into his People by choosing, calling, and leading to himself each individual separately in the unique way appropriate to him...To God's revelation of himself man replies by a free commitment to himself...With this response the human individual enters the

community of the People of God...By abandoning himself
wholly to God the individual at the same time gives himself to
the community of the Church (*SR:* 120, 131, 140).

The identity of ideas here between how Wojtyła understands
Vatican II and how he understands the person in *The Acting Person* is
again manifest. It is because the person is a free self-determining agent
in whom, through conscience, there is an intimate and internal
orientation to truth, that the person can respond to the truth of God.
And it is only because the person can make this response, freely and
wholly, that there can be persons so constituted vertically that they
combine horizontally with each other to form a single people, the
People of God. This directly ties in, as already noted, with Wojtyła's
idea of participation in *The Acting Person*. Participation of one person
with another is only possible because of the individual capacity of self-
determination whereby, through self-gift to each other, they come
together in the sharing, the participating, in a jointly constituted and
jointly lived selfhood. Such participation, properly understood, is never
a loss for the individual person, but rather a perfection and self-
realization. Community and participation are integral to the person. It
is, in fact, in self-giving that the person fulfills himself, as was
emphasized by Wojtyła in *Love and Responsibility*. The same applies to
the reality of faith.

> Man's vocation as a person in a community constitutes the
> basis of the reality of the People of God...*Communio* in fact
> means the actualization of a community in which the
> individual not only preserves his own nature but realizes
> himself definitively...As individuals find themselves in self-
> giving through the interpersonal relationship which we call
> *communio*, so too the individual 'parts' find and affirm
> themselves in the community of the Church...[V]ocation in
> and to the community is the authentic vocation of the person, a
> vocation to fulfill himself or herself (*SR:* 114, 120, 135, 141).

All this is only possible, of course, on the suppositions, first, that
self-gift is an authentically personal act, a genuine realization of the
personal structure of self-determination and, second, that the person is
intrinsically social or communal and intrinsically religious, that is,
summoned to God and to others in the service of God. This human

transcendence to the divine is not discussed or thematized as such in *The Acting Person*. It is hinted at or gestured toward, nevertheless, in the idea of man's vocation to truth and to participation—if, that is, God is genuinely revealed as Truth and as himself Self-Gift in the communion of Persons in the Trinity.

The particular details of all these doctrines, and the particular form that the People of God takes (that it is a visible community and that it has a distinct pattern of authority in an episcopal hierarchy), are not only fully traditional in the way Wojtyła explains them but also go beyond the scope of the present concern. What needs discussion instead is the other part of Wojtyła's analysis of the life of faith, namely that of attitudes. For faith is not just a consciousness, an awareness of who and what one is as a believer; it is also a living out of this consciousness. "Faith without works is dead," says Wojtyła quoting the epistle of St. James (*SR:* 206), and he applies the remark to the need to supplement consciousness (faith as awareness) with attitudes (faith as a principle of, and as issuing in, appropriate deeds). He defines attitude in this context as follows:

> An attitude is an active relationship but it is not yet action. It follows upon cognition and enriched awareness, but is something new and different from these. It involves 'taking up a position' and being ready to act in accordance with it (*SR:* 205).

Applying this to faith, which he had earlier said was a conscious *attitude*, he writes:

> Faith cannot consist merely of knowledge or the content of consciousness. Essential to faith is an attitude of self-commitment to God—a continual readiness to perform the fundamental 'action' which corresponds to the reality of revelation, and all other acts which spring from it and to which it gives their proper character (*SR:* 206).

The action spoken of here is identified by Wojtyła as that of bearing witness to God in all one's life and behavior and in all the complex variety of acts and attitudes that this involves (*SR:* 210). Strengthening the attitude of faith and thereby enabling all believers fully to carry out the fundamental action of faith is what, says Wojtyła,

Vatican II was all about.

Wojtyła goes through a whole discussion of the attitudes proper to the believing People of God (the "People" who, through faith, are "of God" and of each other too). Fundamentally they are all forms or expressions of the attitude of participation in the triple office of Christ as prophet, priest, and king (and here Wojtyła means by "participation" something much more like Plato's idea of sharing in a common property or function than his own idea from *The Acting Person* of constituting a self along with others). In the process of elaborating these attitudes Wojtyła returns frequently to themes from *The Acting Person* (even though he nowhere expressly refers to this work). Let me illustrate with two quotes only from many others, for these quotes go together in defining the attitudes by which the mission, the action of faith, of the People of God is realized in the world.

> [T]he formation of what we call the attitude of 'human identity' [= the attitude of the believer of being in solidarity with all men with whom he lives and to whom he is to bear witness] consists not only in accepting the situation of man in the modern world but in sharing fully in the aspirations which have as their end the true dignity of man. In this way we must discover conscience and the objective moral order to which the human conscience is subordinate (*SR:* 280).

> Responsibility [= the attitude of respect for the dignity of the human person] is closely associated with the dignity of the individual, for it expresses the self-determination—the reverse of willfulness—in which man makes proper use of his freedom by allowing himself to be guided by genuine values and a law of righteousness (*SR:* 291).

One finds in these quotations the themes of participation, self-determination, freedom, the orientation to truth in freedom, conscience, and all as tied to the dignity of man. They have their philosophical roots in *The Acting Person* but they pass over easily and directly into Wojtyła's Christian theology and serve to personalize that philosophy.

There are two general points in these quotations about Wojtyła's approach to the life of faith that are worth noting by way of summary. The first is that he understands this faith on the basis of his phenomenological philosophy of the person, namely on the basis of the

77

structure of self-determination. The second is that his Christian theology, as understood through Vatican II, is likewise thoroughly phenomenological. His focus is on the believer and the community of believers as subjects, and not only or at all as objects. He wishes to analyze and expound the life of faith from the point of view of the lived experience of the believer. That is why, though he covers a lot of traditional ground in theology (so much so that at times one can feel oneself to be reading a theology textbook), he focuses on these things in terms of the believer's interior consciousness and attitudes. His question always is: how do these theological realities (realities that one may have known about since high school catechism) get actualized in the believer, in the structure of his personal self, so that they become formative of his lived experience? This question is obviously not about what it means in terms of a set of propositions or dogmas, but about what it means in terms of living out one's daily life as a believer. What state of mind (or what active consciousness) and what formation of will (or what attitudes) constitute the "what it is like to be a believer" in the Church and in the world? This is, of course, what a classic phenomenological approach to theology would require. The result is that the change, the novelty, in Wojtyła's theological (or even philosophical) thinking is not to be looked for in any new things that are said (Wojtyła does not, and does not try, to propound new doctrines) but in a new way of saying the old and traditional things.

The impression one gets from this book, as from others of Wojtyła, is that everything is both old and yet somehow new in a way that is hard to pin down. One gets contrasting impressions of both familiarity and puzzlement. These things have often been said before, one thinks, so why does Wojtyła not state them plainly like everyone else? But one needs to suspend one's reactions here and try to follow Wojtyła through his own chosen modes of expression. A particular example might help. When speaking of his definition of attitudes (something discussed earlier), Wojtyła says: "In a sense it [an attitude] represents what Thomist psychology would call *habitus* [habit] and even *habitus operativus* [habit of action], but the two are not identical." He does not explain, however, in what way the two are not identical. He simply adds that: "the internal reality that we call an 'attitude' presupposes a fairly precise understanding of man's subjectivity" (*SR:* 205). From this and from what Wojtyła says about subjectivity in *The Acting Person* and elsewhere we may conclude that he is thinking of *habitus* as belonging to metaphysics and the philosophy of being, and of attitude as belonging to phenomenology and the philosophy of consciousness. To sharpen this point, note that *habitus* is properly defined by reference to the soul (a habit is a certain quality of the soul) and that, as such, it fits neatly into Aristotle's Ten Categories. Attitude, by contrast, must belong to the non-Aristotelian category of "lived experience" and is something that is not defined by reference to a category of being but is to be understood by reference to one's own subjectivity and the constitution of one's own selfhood. The attitudes and consciousness of which Wojtyła speaks are the constitutive elements of the believing self, the Christian self. In a sense, therefore, we may say that attitudes and consciousness refer to the same ontological reality as habits and the mental assent to propositions but that they do so in a different way. They do so from the point of view of the lived experience of these realities and not from the point of view of their reduction to more basic categories of being. A *habitus* or a habit, in other words, is, when experienced from within, an attitude, a dimension of one's personal subjectivity. What does a *habitus* feel like, for instance, when we have it and act on the basis of it? Not, to be sure, like a quality of soul even if it is, for "quality of soul" is not expressive of something we subjectively experience; it expresses rather a way of categorizing what lies ontologically behind what we subjectively experience. The way a *habitus* is experienced from within is, perhaps, more like "taking up a position" or a felt "readiness to act" (*SR:* 205). It is like an engagement of our subjective energies, a setting ourselves in place for imminent performance of certain sorts of act. Attitude and consciousness should thus be seen as Wojtyła's way of expressing the abiding and unchanged realities of Christian life and teaching in the form of subjective experience. They are meant to express a phenomenology of believers and the Church as personal subjects forming a communion of personal subjects in the mutual constitution of their lived selves.

Redeeming the Person: The Papal Encyclicals

As Pope John Paul II, Wojtyła has been at the center of some remarkable historical events, most notably the success of the Solidarity Movement in his native Poland and the collapse of Communism in Eastern Europe. Any serious treatment of such events and of John Paul II's political significance in the late Twentieth Century is out of place in a book like this. The interest here is in the philosophical theology of John Paul II as this has manifested itself in his public teaching as pope. For this purpose the focus of attention must be the papal encyclicals.

Encyclicals are, to be sure, not the only official teaching documents issued by popes or with papal authority, but, at least for popes of the last couple of centuries, they are generally the most important such documents.

Encyclicals, as their name indicates, are a sort of "circular." They are open letters sent round or circulated by the pope to the whole Church or, in the case of those of a more restricted interest, to some part of the Church. They are addressed primarily to the bishops, but they can be, and often are, addressed to all the Catholic faithful and to everyone of good will. John Paul II's first encyclical for instance, *Redemptor Hominis*, is addressed to "his venerable brothers in the episcopate, the priests, the religious families, the sons and daughters of the Church, and to all men and women of good will." Encyclicals do not necessarily contain a pope's most important *formal* pronouncements. Paul VI's declaration repeating the Church's teaching against the use of artificial means of birth control was, indeed, promulgated in an encyclical, *Humanae Vitae*, whereas John Paul II's declaration that the Church has no power to ordain women to the priesthood was not so promulgated (it came out in an Apostolic Letter, *Ordinatio Sacerdotalis*). Encyclicals do, nevertheless, tend to contain those teachings, ideas, or proposals that a pope, in his capacity as successor of St. Peter, thinks now most need to be said by the Church to the Church and to the world, in the way in which he thinks they now most need to be said. At any rate that seems to be true of John Paul II. Hence, even if his encyclicals are collaborative works and do not necessarily come in their entirety from his own pen, they can be taken as authentic reflections of his mind. Moreover, in confirmation of this point, it is not hard to see that much of what is said in these encyclicals, and of how it is said too, reflects the philosophical ideas of Karol Wojtyła, especially as these are to be found in *The Acting Person*. In fact, from a philosophical point of view, some of the things said in the encyclicals (as in particular about freedom and truth) make most sense when read in the light of *The Acting Person* and can seem a little puzzling otherwise. At all events, it is from this philosophical perspective that the encyclicals will be discussed here, namely from the point of view of what they tell us about the philosophical theology that Wojtyła's phenomenological personalism has led him to present in his official teaching as John Paul II.

The clue to understanding here is the same as the clue to understanding in the case of Wojtyła's whole philosophy, namely the question of the human person. What the encyclicals give us above all is a *Christological* personalism or a view of the human person from the vantage point of Christ, the God made man. This is a thoroughly theological perspective, of course, since it takes its beginning from revelation and not from unaided reason. But, then, that is exactly how it should be in theological writings, especially the official theological writings of the head of the Church. One should remain alert, nevertheless, as to how philosophical this theology remains, or how thoroughly the data of philosophy are being taken up into and developed by the data of revelation. This becomes evident when one asks what it is about man that John Paul II's Christological personalism brings to the fore. The answer (as is already made clear in his first encyclical, *Redemptor Hominis*) is that it is the dignity of man as made in the image of God and as restored to that image by Christ. Furthermore, this dignity of man is identified as his transcendence, his standing above all other created things, including his own physical nature, and his being directed or called to a super-creaturely life in God.

Transcendence here is understood pretty much as it is in *The Acting Person*, namely man's freedom, his capacity to determine himself and not to be determined by anything extrinsic to himself (by objects or passions or forces). But there is a difference, the difference of revelation. For revelation shows several further things. First, man was made by God in God's own image so that his transcendence is a mirror of the transcendence of the Deity. Second, God took up that image in the Incarnation and united it with himself in the Person of the Son, so that human reality is disclosed as being so much at one with divine reality as to be fit to be ontologically united with the very Godhead itself. Third, through Christ, the Incarnate Son, all men are called to share really and personally in that same life of God so that human transcendence finds its ultimate in lived experience to be the lived experience of God. Fourth, and finally, human beings not only have such an exalted beginning and such an exalted destiny, but also their transcendence and capacity for exaltation have been gravely damaged by some deep, original fault that runs counter to the Creator's work and afflicts each and every man in his being and in his experience. The creature has somehow rebelled against the Creator, denied his dependence, and rejected the relation of friendship and love that the Creator offers.

We face here in this last case the Church's traditional teaching of Original Sin. But the disobedience to God that is this Original Sin is not only a rebellion against the Creator; it is also a rebellion against the creature. It is man's denial, in effect, of his own creatureliness, his own dependence on God for being, truth, goodness, beauty. John Paul II asserts this doctrine on the basis of Scripture texts and most especially the *Book of Genesis*, but it is a doctrine that is, in many ways, an extension also of the philosophy of *The Acting Person*. Take, for instance, this quotation from *Dominum et Vivificantem* (sect. 36):

> Man cannot decide by himself what is good and what is evil—cannot "know good and evil, like God." In the created world *God* indeed remains the first and sovereign source *for deciding about good and evil*, through the intimate truth of being, which is the reflection of the *Word*, the eternal Son, consubstantial with the Father. To man, created to the image of God, the Holy Spirit gives the gift of *conscience*, so that in this conscience the image may faithfully reflect its model, which is both Wisdom and eternal Law, the source of the moral order in man and in the world. "Disobedience," as the original dimension of sin, means *the rejection of this source*, through man's claim to become an independent and exclusive source for deciding about good and evil.

We are presented here with standard Christian theology, but the expression of this theology recalls fundamental themes of *The Acting Person*, namely truth and conscience. For *The Acting Person*, in its explorations at the level of unaided reason, displayed, within the structure of the person, man's radical orientation toward objective truth, a truth whose dynamic meaning for action, its force as norm and duty, is mediated through conscience. All that the text from *Dominum et Vivificantem* does—which is by no means trivial of course—is to personalize more radically this structure from *The Acting Person*. The truth to which the person is structurally ordered is not some abstract fact or set of propositions but itself a Person, the Person of the Word, the Son of God. And conscience, which mediates this truth, is not just an inner moment of the person's self but a gift from the Holy Spirit, so that through conscience and acceptance of the Truth the person may faithfully reflect the image to which he was made, the image of God. The structure of the person, his transcendence toward truth and his power of determining himself in the truth, remains exactly as it was already set out in *The Acting Person*. Only now it is seen in a supernaturally revealed light and with a supernaturally revealed meaning. We hereby come to learn that the dignity of man is an altogether surpassing one, that it is the dignity of being the image of the Divine Trinity—an image, moreover, who is, in his acting, intimately moved by and to that Trinity. We are also at the same time brought to learn the surpassing evil of sin, that it destroys or damages, not the inner structure of the person only (in the way that *The Acting Person* and also *Love and Responsibility* already explored), but the image of the Trinity, and that, in addition, sin is an offense, not merely against some rule or norm of conscience, but against a Person, the Person of the Holy Spirit and, through him, also against the Son and the Father.

That is why John Paul II affirms, in the words of Vatican II, that only Christ "fully reveals man to himself and brings to light his most high calling" (*Redemptor Hominis:* sect. 8, quoting *Gaudium et Spes:* sect. 22). Or as he says again:

> In Christ and through Christ man has acquired full awareness of his dignity, of the heights to which he is raised, of the surpassing worth of his humanity, and of the meaning of his existence (*Redemptor Hominis:* sect. 11).

The theme of the dignity of man, already stressed on purely natural grounds in *The Acting Person* and *Love and Responsibility*, thus becomes, in the encyclicals and on the basis of revelation, the theme of the divinization of man through Christ. The two together—human dignity and Christ the perfect man who fully reveals that dignity—become the measure of everything else that John Paul II says. They constitute the essence of his theology, his philosophical theology, and nothing much makes sense without them.

It is, for instance, a cardinal thesis of John Paul II, repeated in several encyclicals, that to separate freedom from truth is a grave error, perhaps the gravest error of our times. Freedom is necessarily tied to truth, or truth makes us free, because it is truth that preserves us in our transcendence and prevents us from denying this human dignity, whether in ourselves or others.

> *[O]bedience to the truth* about God and man is the first condition of freedom, making it possible for a person to order his needs and desires and to choose the means of satisfying them according to a correct scale of values...If one does not acknowledge transcendent truth, then the force of power takes

over, and each person tends to make full use of the means at his disposal in order to impose his own interests or his own opinion, with no regard for the rights of others...In a world without truth, freedom loses its foundation and man is exposed to the violence of passion and manipulation, both open and hidden (*Centesimus Annus:* sects. 41, 44, 46).

To be subject to the power of passion and selfish interest, whether in oneself or others, is to lose one's transcendence, one's capacity for self-determination. It is to be determined by something other, by something that merely happens in or to one, and no longer to be the true agent of one's own acts. To be free is, instead, to yield only to truth in one's action and to let nothing deter one from yielding only to truth. It is not easy to do this; it is not easy to control oneself so that only truth rules. It is not easy, in other words, to live free. That is why John Paul II repeats that it is for freedom that Christ has set us free, namely that he has set us free from our dominance by lesser things and restored to us the power and the will to give ourselves instead to the higher things that are Truth and Goodness.

Reason and experience not only confirm the weakness of human freedom; they also confirm its tragic aspects. Man comes to realize that his freedom is in some mysterious way inclined to betray this openness to the True and the Good, and that all too often he actually prefers to choose finite, limited and ephemeral goods. What is more, within his errors and his negative decisions, man glimpses the source of a deep rebellion, which leads him to reject the Truth and the Good... Consequently, *freedom needs to be set free. It is Christ who sets us free (Veritatis Splendor:* sect. 86).

Freedom is free when the person uses his freedom to give himself to truth and, in so giving, to find himself free from all that is not true and not good. Such self-giving to truth is, when seen in the light of revelation, self-giving to Truth, to Christ the Incarnate Son of God. It is transcendence divinized.

John Paul II sees the Virgin Mary as the great example of such self-gift to Truth:

[A]t the Annunciation Mary entrusted herself to God

completely, with "the full submission of intellect and will," manifesting "the obedience of faith" to him who spoke to her through his messenger. She responded, therefore, *with all her human and feminine "I,"* and this response of faith included both perfect cooperation with "the grace of God that precedes and assists" and perfect openness to the action of the Holy Spirit (*Redemptoris Mater:* sect. 13).

One notes about this quotation that the phrase about Mary responding *with all her human and feminine "I"* has its philosophical origin in the phenomenology of *The Acting Person,* and best makes philosophical sense in the light of the analysis given there (and in *Love and Responsibility*) of the idea of self-gift, the gift of one "I" to another "I."

Because Truth is thus the safeguard and the object of human freedom, John Paul II can roundly criticize and reject all competing notions of freedom which see it as an absolute independence from truth and from objective norms; that see it as man creating his own good and evil for himself, as being his own source of values. Such "freedom" is really a sort of tyranny of the strong. John Paul II sees evidence for this above all in what he calls the modern "culture of death" with its attacks on the weak, the poor, the defenseless, the marginalized of all kinds. He speaks of "a completely individualistic concept of freedom, which ends up by becoming the freedom of the strong against the weak who have no choice but to submit." Or again, in the same place:

> [F]reedom negates and destroys itself and becomes a factor leading to the destruction of others when it no longer recognizes and respects *its essential link with the truth.* When freedom, out of a desire to emancipate itself from all forms of tradition and authority, shuts out even the most obvious evidence of an objective and universal truth, which is the foundation of personal and social life, then the person ends up by no longer taking as the sole and indisputable point of reference for his own choices the truth about good and evil, but only his subjective and changeable opinion or, indeed, his selfish interest and whim (*Evangelium Vitae:* sect. 19).

Of course it is the opinions and whims of the powerful that in fact prevail when this is the case and hence freedom becomes slavery for the weak and arbitrary willfulness for the strong, which are both the denial of freedom since in neither case is human transcendence realized or respected. Furthermore, democracy, the alleged rule of freedom for all, becomes in fact a totalitarianism, a tyrant state which:

> arrogates to itself the right to dispose of the life of the weakest and most defenseless members, from the unborn child to the elderly, in the name of a public interest which is really nothing but the interest of one part...[W]hen freedom is detached from objective truth it becomes impossible to establish personal rights on a firm and rational basis; and the ground is laid for society to be at the mercy of the unrestrained will of individuals or the oppressive totalitarianism of public authority (*Evangelium Vitae:* sects. 20, 96).

The safeguard of freedom is truth and the absolute norm of truth which means, above all, the absolute norm of respect for the dignity and equal rights of all without discrimination. It is an error, therefore, to see moral absolutes as the enemy of freedom and of the person. They are the very reverse:

> Because there can be no freedom apart from or in opposition to the truth, the categorical—unyielding and uncompromising—defense of the absolutely essential demands of man's personal dignity must be considered the way and the condition for the very existence of freedom (*Veritatis Splendor:* sect. 96).

This is, of course, a re-assertion of the personalistic norm from *Love and Responsibility*. But John Paul II sees this norm as preserved by theism and as effectively denied by atheism. It is religious faith and the revelation of God that preserves and enhances the dignity of man, while the denial of God leads, in the end, to the denial of that dignity.

> In seeking the deepest roots of the struggle between the "culture of life" and the "culture of death," we cannot restrict ourselves to the perverse idea of freedom mentioned above [the idea of freedom as "an *absolute power over others and against others*"]. We have to go the heart of the tragedy being experienced by modern man: *the eclipse of the sense of God*

and of man...[W]hen the sense of God is lost, there is also a tendency to lose the sense of man, of his dignity and his life... (*Evangelium Vitae:* sect. 21).

The attacks on life through abortion and euthanasia are particular cases in point. These are direct denials of the personalistic norm, of course, but, because of the truth about man disclosed in revelation, they are also direct denials of the God in whose image man was made and to whose image Christ has restored him. There is no use pleading here that not all human beings are persons because 'person' means someone with consciousness or the capacity for communication or the like which the unborn and the very old lack. John Paul II speaks of this idea as:

> the mentality which *carries the concept of subjectivity to an extreme* and even distorts it, and recognizes as a subject of rights only the person who enjoys full or at least incipient autonomy and who emerges from a state of total dependence on others. But how can we reconcile this approach with *the exaltation of man as a being who is "not to be used"?* (*Evangelium Vitae:* sect. 19).

We can see implicit here the whole of John Paul II's polemic, as Karol Wojtyła, against the subjectivism of the philosophy of consciousness—that philosophy which fails to see, or denies, the objective reality of the person in the *suppositum humanum*, even when this reality is manifested from within conscious experience itself. Properly understood, 'person' is not, contrary to what some contemporary philosophers claim, a property-term indicating the actual presence of consciousness or autonomy or communication or the like. It is a substance-term indicating a certain kind of real existent, a certain kind of suppositum. That is why abortion and euthanasia and all such deeds, even when their objects are not yet or no longer capable of action or thought or speech, are direct killings of persons, direct denials of human rights. That is why it is atheism, and not religion as many claim, that is the destructive and alienating factor in human life. The truth about man, his self-determining transcendence over all earthly things, the ordination of his freedom to objective good—all these get cast into doubt or denied when God is denied. It is the Church, with its constant and unfailing teaching of the revealed truth, that saves the person from self-destruction, and that saves freedom and conscience too (*Dominum et Vivificantem:* sects. 37-38, 44, 47).

But the restoration of persons to individual wholeness through Christ also requires, and prepares the way for, the restoration of the community of persons, or state and society, to wholeness. For here again the denial of the truth about man is tied up with the denial of God. The error of socialism, and of capitalism, is to be traced back to atheism, explicit or implicit. This error is, in the first place, an anthropological error. It is, in socialism's case, the error of reducing man to an element of society instead of treating him as an ontological subject (a suppositum) with the capacity for free self-determination, as "an autonomous subject of moral decision."

> It is by responding to the call of God contained in the being of things that man became aware of his transcendent dignity. Every individual must give this response, which constitutes the apex of his humanity, and no social mechanism or collective subject can substitute for it (*Centesimus Annus:* sect. 13).

But capitalism too, the capitalism of the first world, is guilty of a like fault, a like denial of the dignity of man. For advanced capitalist societies have turned people away from their authentic personhood to the consumerism of "a web of false and superficial gratifications" or have organized work so as to maximize profit with no concern whether the worker, through his labor, grows or diminishes as a person, whether he is treated, and treats himself, as an end and not as a means.

> The concept of alienation needs to be led back to the Christian vision of reality, by recognizing in alienation a reversal of means and ends...Man is alienated if he refuses to transcend himself and to live the experience of self-giving and of the formation of an authentic human community oriented toward his final destiny, which is God (*Centesimus Annus:* sect. 41).

A true and just society must take the dignity of man as its basis and its goal, and must serve man instead of making man serve it or things or profit. For this reason society must respect the rights of the person, the equal rights of all persons. These rights include, for instance: the right to life, especially the right of the child to develop in its mother's womb; the right to live in a united family and a moral environment conducive to the growth of the child's personality; the right to develop one's intelligence and freedom in seeking and knowing truth; the right to share in work which makes wise use of the earth's resources; the right freely to establish a family through the responsible use of one's sexuality; and finally, as the source and synthesis of these rights, religious freedom or the right to live in the truth of one's faith and in conformity with one's transcendent dignity as a person (*Centesimus Annus:* sect. 47).

As part and parcel of all this are the principles of solidarity and participation, which John Paul II is taking, not only from documents of previous popes, but also, of course, from his own work in *The Acting Person.* Fully in line with that work, solidarity is understood as "*a firm and persevering determination* to commit oneself to the *common good*; that is to say to the good of all and of each individual" (*Sollicitudo Rei Socialis:* sect. 38). Similarly, participation is understood as the sharing of each in the making of decisions, in determining common life together. It is, in short, what participation is in *The Acting Person,* namely the joint exercise and realization of the structure of self-determination (*Redemptor Hominis:* sect. 17; *Centesimus Annus:* sects. 35, 43, 46; *Laborem Exercens:* sects. 8, 15). It is tied to the further principle of subsidiarity. This principle, which can be found, to be sure, in other papal documents, cannot be found, in so many words, in *The Acting Person.* Nevertheless John Paul II gives it a personalist interpretation fully in harmony with that book. He calls it the "subjectivity" of society and identifies it with the "creation of structures of participation and shared responsibility" (*Centesimus Annus:* sect. 46). In other words, he understands it as a principle designed to ensure as much participation by individuals in the determination of their lives as possible. He applies it specifically to the modern Welfare State, or Social Assistance State, which, despite good intentions and some good results, has effectively rejected this principle.

> By intervening directly and depriving society of its responsibility, the Social Assistance State leads to a loss of human energies and an inordinate increase of public agencies, which are dominated more by bureaucratic ways of thinking than by concern for serving their clients (*Centesimus Annus:* sect. 48).

It is clear that, in the name of the person, John Paul II favors a definite emphasis on devolution and decentralization in modern states.

All such social policies and recommendations are, he claims, in the service of authentic development. For authentic development is the development of persons, not of things or products or mechanisms.

> Development...must be measured and oriented according to the reality and vocation of man seen in his totality, namely in his *interior dimension*...[I]n trying to achieve true development we must never lose sight of that *dimension* which is in the *specific nature* of man, who has been created by God in his image and likeness...[D]evelopment cannot consist only in the use, dominion over, and *indiscriminate* possession of created things and the products of human industry, but rather in *subordinating* the possession, dominion, and use to man's divine likeness and to his vocation to immortality. This is the *transcendent reality* of the human being... (*Sollicitudo Rei Socialis:* sect. 29).

That is why the heart and soul of development is evangelization, or spreading the good news about man's transcendence and his redemption in Christ. The Church is an "expert in humanity" and her "first contribution to the solution of the urgent problem of development" is to proclaim "the truth about Christ, about herself, and about man" (*Sollicitudo Rei Socialis:* sect. 41; *Redemptoris Missio:* sect. 58). Accordingly, not only is it the case that the Church has the *right* to evangelize, but it is also the case that all peoples have a *right* to be evangelized, the right "to hear the 'Good News' of the God who reveals and gives himself in Christ, so that each one can live out in its fullness his or her proper calling" (*Redemptoris Missio:* sect. 46). Or again:

> [A] people's development does not derive primarily from money, material assistance, or technological means, but from the formation of consciences and the gradual maturing of ways of thinking and patterns of behavior. *Man is the principal agent of development*, not money or technology. The Church forms consciences by revealing to peoples the God whom they seek and do not yet know, the grandeur of man created in God's image and loved by him, the equality of all men and women as God's sons and daughters...(*Redemptoris Missio:* sect. 58).

90

Such evangelization is not tyranny or imperialism. On the contrary it is the making possible for all persons what is already present in all persons from the beginning, whether they realize it or not. Referring back to the Second Vatican Council, John Paul II says that the presence and activity of the Spirit of God are universal, not limited by or to space and time. God's Spirit is at work in the heart of every person through the "seeds of the word" that are to be found in all human initiatives, including religious ones, and "in mankind's efforts to attain truth, goodness, and God himself" (*Redemptoris Missio:* sect. 28). One should add, therefore, that philosophy too is one of these initiatives, one of these efforts—the philosophy that throughout history and in all cultures and in many different ways has been the manifestation of man's search for wisdom through the exercise of reason. But reason is only one of the "wings" by which man rises to the divine. The other wing is faith, faith in Christ who is Wisdom Incarnate and who opens up to reason a scope and a range and a fulfillment that would not otherwise be possible. Evangelization, therefore, is part of the development of philosophy. Moreover today especially it is a summons to philosophy not to give up its sapiential dimension, its pursuit of wisdom, and not to give way to suspicion or despair. For philosophy too, like everything proper to the person, needs to be redeemed from what in it tends to the denial of the person's transcendence and dignity (*Fides et Ratio:* ch. 7).

As prime examples of evangelization, John Paul II cites Saints Cyril and Methodius who brought the gospel to the Slav nations and showed, through their love for the Slavs and their respect for Slav heritage, how the gospel enhances and supports indigenous culture and enables it to achieve greater authentic development than it would or could have achieved on its own. For though Cyril and Methodius were Greeks by birth and training, yet in their missionary work they were "Slavs at heart" (*Slavorum Apostoli:* sect. 12). Notable in this regard is the new alphabet Cyril devised for expressing the unique sounds of the Slav language (called "Cyrillic" to this day), and which he and Methodius then used to translate the scriptures into Slavonic.

> [T]hey set themselves to understanding and penetrating the language, customs, and traditions of the Slav peoples, faithfully interpreting the aspirations and human values which were present and expressed therein (*Slavorum Apostoli:* sect. 10).

John Paul II, we may say, regards the evangelizing Church as the true preserver and promoter of culture—of each and every culture in all its uniqueness—and thus as the true multicultural force in the world, the true pluralist society.

> The Gospel does not lead to the impoverishment or extinction of those things which every individual, people, and nation and every culture throughout history recognizes and brings into being as goodness, truth, and beauty. On the contrary, it strives to assimilate and to develop these values: to live them with magnanimity and joy and to perfect them by the mysterious and ennobling light of revelation (*Slavorum Apostoli:* sect. 18).

The Church is Catholic because she embraces truth, goodness, and beauty everywhere, because she is thus truly inclusive and pluralist and yet brings everything into a peaceful and harmonious unity founded on the Truth that is Christ—the universal and eternal Truth that never fades but preserves, enhances, and perfects the personal dignity of all men always and everywhere.

This is a grand vision, to be sure, and controversial. It is nevertheless a thoroughly Catholic vision, in line with the tradition of the Church's teaching throughout the centuries. It also displays a striking consistency with everything Karol Wojtyła has said on the question of man from his first explorations of moral philosophy, through his phenomenological personalism in *The Acting Person* and *Love and Responsibility*, and into his reading of the Second Vatican Council and his papal encyclicals. For if the claims, made above all in *The Acting Person*, about the transcendence and integration of the human person are true, and if Christ is he who fully reveals man to himself in revealing this transcendence as an aboriginal vocation to the divine, then the claims that John Paul II makes about rights, development, the social question, evangelization, and the Church all more or less follow as a matter of internal necessity. Wojtyła's thought from beginning to end, from the lecture hall to the pulpit, from the philosopher's chair to the Chair of Peter, displays a coherence, a scope, and a humanism that are remarkable. One may disagree, of course, and I suppose many will. But it would be hard not to admire.

Bibliography

This bibliography contains only works referred to in the text. A full bibliography can be found in George Weigel's *Witness to Hope*. His book and Buttiglione's are good places to start for those who want to learn more about Wojtyła's life and thought. Of Wojtyła's own philosophical works *Love and Responsibility* is the most accessible. *Person and Community* is the next most accessible and will facilitate the understanding of *The Acting Person* which can otherwise be tough going. Of the encyclicals, *Fides et Ratio* and *Evangelium Vitae* are probably the best ones for the philosophically minded to begin with.

A. Works by Wojtyła/John Paul II

Wojtyła, Karol. *The Acting Person*. Translated by Andrzej Potocki and edited by Anna-Teresa Tymieniecka. Dordrecht: D. Reidel Publishing Company, 1979.

_____. *Love and Responsibility*. Translated by H. T. Willetts. San Francisco: Ignatius Press, 1993.

_____. *Person and Community: Selected Essays*. Translated by Theresa Sandok. New York: Peter Lang, 1993

_____. *Sources of Renewal: The Implementation of Vatican II*. Translated by F. S. Falla. San Francisco: Harper and Row, 1980.

John Paul II. *The Papal Encyclicals of John Paul II*. Edited with introductions by J. Michael Miller, C.S.B. Huntington, Indiana: Our Sunday Visitor, 1996.

_____. *Fides et Ratio*. Vatican Translation. Boston: Pauline Books, 1998.

B. Works about Wojtyła/John Paul II

Buttiglione, Rocco. *Karol Wojtyła. The Thought of the Man Who Became John Paul II*. Translated by Paolo Guietti and Francesca Murphy. Grand Rapids: Eerdmans, 1997.

Kalinowski, George. 'La Pensée Philosophique de Karol Wojtyła et la Faculté de Philosophie de l'Université Catholique de Lublin,' in *Aletheia* 4 (1988): 198-216.

Weigel, George. *Witness to Hope. The Biography of John Paul II*. New York: HarperCollins, 1999.